50 Brilliant Minds
of the Last 100 Years

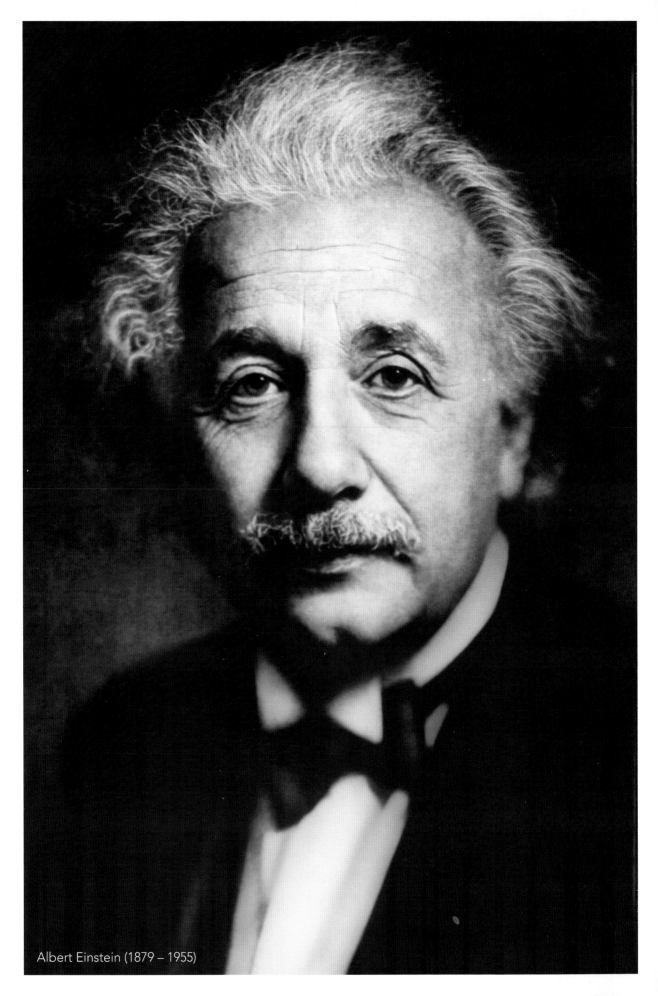

Albert Einstein (1879 – 1955)

50 Brilliant Minds of the Last 100 Years

Identifying the Mystery of Genius

Rodney Castleden

CHARTWELL
BOOKS

CONTENTS

PREFACE

We sometimes meet people who seem to possess a quality of mind that is completely out of the ordinary – a mind that is outstanding in its penetration, perhaps wayward and going off along unfamiliar paths, coming up with what sound like brand-new ideas. We sense that these people are brilliant, but I think most of us would be hard pressed to explain exactly how we know that.

How do we, how *can* we, identify a brilliant mind? Some commentators define a genius as someone with a very high intelligence quotient: an IQ test-measured at 140 or over according to some, or 160 or more according to others. This means that some lists of geniuses exclude Albert Einstein, who is said to have had an IQ lower than 160. But many people would argue, and I think rightly, that in any case a high IQ on its own is not enough. Someone who is equipped with an incredible learning capacity or memory or potential for complex thought may in fact not have an original thought in their head. Or they may simply fail to use their astonishing brain power, because of laziness or complacency – they may lack drive. They may not contribute in any way to the furtherance of human knowledge. They may do little or nothing to expand our horizons as a race.

The 19th century poet Samuel Taylor Coleridge came perilously close to this situation. Most people who met the youthful Coleridge thought him a brilliant and amazing young man who was destined for great things, but in adulthood his opium habit got the better of him and he ended up massively under-achieving. Even Dorothy Wordsworth, who loved Coleridge dearly, commented that there was no point in Coleridge's endlessly filling his head with reading if he never got round to *using* his knowledge by writing.

Another of Coleridge's problems was that he saw his friend Wordsworth as by far the better poet and he continually allowed Wordsworth's writing career to dominate his own. People who have very high intellectual potential, but for one reason or another do not harness it, may not do anything at all. And if that is so, it is hard to see how they can be regarded as geniuses, or even how we would tell that they had brilliant minds. The brilliant minds selected for inclusion in this book are paradigm-shifters, people who have actually changed the world or changed the way we see it. The acid-test has to be the *achievement*.

A genius has exceptional intellectual ability, creativity and originality. But he or she also has to take action, to have drive, determination and persistence in order to achieve a result. A genius does amazing things that have never been done before, things that take the human race a step forward.

How have the 50 people described in this book been selected? The focus is very much on the 20th and early 21st centuries – the times we live in now and the times our parents and grandparents lived through. This has meant that a lot of the brilliant minds of earlier generations will *not* be making an appearance here: Pythagoras, Michelangelo, Shakespeare, Newton, Bach, Voltaire – none of them will be found here. Taking their places are Einstein, Picasso, Le Corbusier, Joyce, Hubble, Miles Davis and Bertrand Russell. But even limiting the list to the last hundred years or so has meant excluding a lot of very remarkable people. The selection is intended to be representative of a wide range of disciplines: astronomy, physics, chemistry, mathematics, literature, biology, medicine, psychology, music, film, electronics and computers, philosophy, art, architecture, laser technology, economics and mass culture. We could probably nominate 50 remarkable achievers in each of those areas.

One popular idea is that intelligence and high achievement are hereditary. There are some geniuses who do indeed come from high-achieving families, or at least families where the parents have highly developed skills in the same area, like Niels Bohr, Max Planck, Pablo Picasso, Ludwig Wittgenstein and Tim Berners-Lee. But there are also some geniuses who come from very ordinary backgrounds, from families where there is no sign of what is to come, like Irving Berlin, Walt Disney, Jean-Paul Sartre, Flossie Wong-Staal and James Lovelock. These people seem to come out of nowhere, like burning bright comets.

It has often been assumed that geniuses are a race apart, different from the rest of us. I hope that this book goes some way towards showing that this is by no means the case. The 'brilliant' are in many ways ordinary people like us, facing the ordinary problems of everyday life. Some of them, like Max Planck, even find the extraordinary new ideas they give birth to an unwanted problem in their lives. Many of those included in this book had to struggle to make a living, like James Joyce and Igor Stravinsky, in order to pursue their new ideas. Many had to cope with adversity of one kind or another.

Most of us would struggle to write a convincing novel in our first language, but Joseph Conrad managed to write several great novels in his third language. Max Planck had to cope with repeated bereavement, finally and most poignantly when his beloved son Erwin was executed by the Gestapo for trying to kill Hitler. Marie Curie was deprived first of her lover, then of her husband, and had to struggle to overcome despair. Grace Hopper managed to overcome gender prejudice in order to make her way in the 'man's world' of the US Navy. In a similar way, Percy Julian managed to overcome racial prejudice. Andy Warhol worked with a poor physical

constitution further weakened by a serious gunshot injury. The writer Jorge Luis Borges somehow coped with blindness; Stephen Hawking has achieved on a very high level in spite of disabling motor neurone disease. An enormous quantum of positive energy is required to achieve great things against adversity on this scale – but it happens, and amazingly it happens again and again.

Geniuses also have negative characteristics, or personality flaws, just like the rest of us. Inevitably, among high achievers, a common one is a tendency to grab the credit. With that goes a failure to acknowledge help, often on a large scale, from other people; the songwriter Irving Berlin persistently failed to acknowledge his arrangers, wanting to take all the credit for the music. Some have gone as far as taking other people's work in order to succeed. But there are huge variations. Some may be seen as vain or arrogant, like Edwin Hubble, others are surprisingly modest, humble and self-effacing, like Enrico Fermi and Jean-Paul Sartre.

The range of human failings that geniuses show should give us ordinary people heart. If they, the geniuses, with all their flaws, problems and setbacks, are able to achieve great things, then maybe we too, in our small way, can achieve something. We should at least aspire to achievement. We can never know unless we try.

A high proportion of the people featured here were, when young, very strongly supported by their parents, either because of their professional backgrounds and consequent inside knowledge or because of their willingness to give moral and financial support. Examples include Ludwig Wittgenstein, Miles Davis and John Maynard Keynes. But some high-achieving men and women are self-made, they have come from financially poor families, or parents who lack the cultural background to give appropriate support; Sigmund Freud, James Joyce, Irving Berlin, James Lovelock and Andy Warhol fall into this group of self-made men. So – many high achievers are vigorously helped on their way by their parents, but a minority make their own determined way.

Some of the people included here come into the category of genius as it was brilliantly and memorably defined by the American inventor Thomas Edison: 'One per cent inspiration, ninety-nine per cent perspiration.' Two of the women included have worked like this – achieving great things by persistent, painstaking hard work – Jocelyn Bell and Flossie Wong-Staal. The shortage of women in this list of *50 Brilliant Minds* is noticeable and worrying, and it may

be that the story of Jocelyn Bell Burnell is an indication of what has been going on. She is an example of a high-achieving woman who has not been appropriately recognized at least in part because she was a woman; the men associated with her project were awarded a Nobel Prize, but she was not. She has also commented that she was conditioned to think that her work should not be acknowledged. Are there perhaps other women in history who have been elbowed aside in this way, intimidated into

Apple Computer co-founders
Steve Wozniak (left) and Steve Jobs.

taking the back-seat? Certainly Marie Curie was well aware that she had continually to fight against this kind of treatment in a world (then) dominated by men.

Have we perhaps in the past overlooked geniuses, whether because they were female or because they were beta or gamma males, people who were shouldered aside by those who were more assertive, more hungry, more determined to take credit? It was certainly the case with the great English scientist Robert Hooke. He made an enemy of Isaac Newton, and Newton did everything he could to annihilate Hooke's reputation. And he almost succeeded; today it is Isaac Newton we remember, and few people have even heard of Robert Hooke.

And do we perhaps today wrongly credit people with brilliance because they have made colossal amounts of money? An element of the awe that we feel for Bill Gates is to do with his commercial power, and with his phenomenal wealth. We perhaps admire Steve Jobs because his personal fortune in the year before his death amounted to more than 8 billion dollars. The co-founder of Apple, Steve Wozniak, amassed net wealth that was estimated in 2010 to be one per cent of that, and *his* name is rarely mentioned by comparison – yet it was Wozniak's brilliance that produced the design for the Apple computer, not Jobs. Are we more impressed by the computer, or the wealth? Whatever the answer, it says more about us than it does about Steve Jobs or Steve Wozniak.

Perhaps we attach a higher value to the entrepreneur than to the creator. And perhaps we should question whether we have got it right. In the body of the book I have tried hard to keep value judgements out, to let the reader decide what sort of people these are, but sometimes it has been difficult. I am aware that, in the piece about the philosopher Ludwig Wittgenstein, I have been unable to conceal my view of the man!

Some geniuses are visionaries, and it is possible to see Gandhi, Robert Goddard, Nelson Mandela and even Andy Warhol as visionaries. Some geniuses are misguided visionaries, people with a vision that is fundamentally flawed, like Le Corbusier or Arnold Schoenberg. Some have one brilliant idea, like Max Planck, others have one brilliant idea after another, like Roger Penrose. Still others have visions and then later have doubts about them, like Einstein, Hubble and Lovelock.

A theme that I hope will emerge strikingly from this review of just a selection of the great minds of the 20th and 21st century is their enormous diversity. The reader may like to think of other candidates for inclusion – certainly there could be another 50, and another. The book does not try to put these great minds in order or separate them into their specialist subjects – it is not a chart or hit parade. Instead it runs in an egalitarian alphabetic order providing the reader with intriguing pairings where Einstein follows Edison, Gates follows Gandhi and Matisse follows Mandela. I leave the reader to judge who among the collection is the greatest.

The richness and vitality of our civilization is largely down to these dreamers of dreams, these movers of mountains, these game changers. Just looking at this selection of 50 men and women, it is astonishing to think how much they have achieved, how much they have advanced our civilization. They introduced us to surreal literature, modern jazz and 12-tone music, abstract art, a variety of new philosophies including existentialism, personal computers and the Internet, relativity, black holes and galaxies outside our own, HIV, the structure of DNA, psychoanalysis, electric lights, feature-length cartoon films, passive resistance, rockets and a variety of alternative visions of the future. These – and many more inventions and new ideas – sprang from the brilliant minds of just 50 people, the 50 in this book, and each of them represents a very special achievement.

"If you knew how much work went into it, you wouldn't call it genius."

Michelangelo Buonarrotti

JOCELYN BELL BURNELL

In Pursuit of Pulsars and Extraterrestrials

QUOTE

"Scientists should never claim that something is absolutely true. You should never claim perfect, or total, or 100% because you never ever get there."

BIOGRAPHY

NAME: Susan Jocelyn Bell Burnell

BORN: July 15, 1943
Belfast, Northern Ireland,
United Kingdom

NATIONALITY: Northern Irish / British

OCCUPATION: Astronomer, astrophysicist

The astrophysicist Jocelyn Bell, now Professor Dame Jocelyn Bell Burnell, was born in Belfast, close to the Armagh Observatory in Northern Ireland. She was brought up within a Quaker family and, when she failed to gain a place at a grammar school by way of the 11-plus exam, her parents decided to send her to the Mount School, the Quaker girls' school in York, England. She earned a BSc degree in physics at Glasgow, Scotland in 1965 and then gained a PhD degree at Cambridge University, England in 1969.

It was while she was a PhD student at Cambridge that Jocelyn Bell Burnell made a discovery that changed the way we see the universe. Hailed as the greatest astronomical discovery of the 20th century, she found a new and entirely unexpected family of stars – the pulsars. The existence of pulsars – dense cores of collapsed stars that emit pulsating radio waves – suddenly made black holes seem much more likely and provided further proof to Einstein's theory of gravity.

For a long time people had speculated that there might be advanced civilizations elsewhere in the universe and that we might be able to pick up radio signals sent by them, perhaps in a deliberate attempt to make contact. Jocelyn Bell picked up a very regular radio signal, an uninterrupted series of regular blips, from one part of the sky, and it looked conceivable to her and her supervisor, Antony Hewish, that this might be the long-awaited signal from the aliens … 'the Little Green Men'.

It would have been a major discovery in itself. But then the telescope was pointed at a completely different part of the night sky, and she got the same result again. She was watching at 2 or 3 in the morning on a very cold December night in 1974. On the recorder she saw the same regular pulse every few seconds, blip, blip, blip as before, evidently from the same family of objects as before. She knew this was very unlikely to be a signal from Little Green Men, because it came from another part of the universe, and it was scarcely possible that two LGM civilizations, from different star systems, would be using similar equipment to transmit exactly the same message on the same radio frequency.

The regularity of the signal was completely unexpected and had never been dreamt of before. Jocelyn Bell knew that she had discovered a previously unknown natural phenomenon, and a new class of object that must be producing it. This repeat discovery was sufficient to persuade her supervisors and the senior staff in her department, that a major discovery had been made. Martin Ryle alerted the editor of the prestigious science journal *Nature* that major news was on the way, the discovery of a totally new kind of object. The paper describing the discovery had five named authors, of whom Antony Hewish was the first. The new object was a pulsar, a spinning neutron star releasing jets of radio signals from its poles.

Throughout history some theories have been enduring, standing the test of time well, while other theories have been short-lived because they have been tested and failed. Einstein's theory of relativity has been subjected to a lot of scrutiny over the last century, and so far it has stood up well. But it is only with the discovery of pulsars that Einstein's ideas on gravitation have been proved correct. If two stars orbit round one another they will tend to produce gravitational waves, and travel faster and faster as they move together. The actions of binary star systems seem to prove that Einstein was right.

But scientists should never claim total truth, because they can never, ever, reach the total truth. Science, Jocelyn believes, is the search for understanding, rather than the search for absolute truth. A search for understanding is more serviceable to mankind, and a sufficiently ambitious goal.

"If we assume we've arrived; we stop searching, we stop developing."

Jocelyn Bell has a clear view of science and how it works, or rather how it should work. Sometimes science goes backwards rather than forwards. She compares it to doing a Rubik cube; sometimes you have to make more of a mess before you can get it right. Sometimes, in order to make progress, you have to abandon a long-cherished view of the universe, which scientists are generally reluctant to do. She quotes as an example the view that scholars in the middle ages developed about the solar system. They thought the planets had to travel in perfect circles; because they were heavenly bodies their geometry had to be divinely perfect.

When they saw that the movements of the planets did not follow perfect circles, they added epicycles, small circles within the larger circular orbits, to explain the aberrations. When the gradually improving telescope showed that even these epicycles could not explain the planets' paths, they invented further epicycles. The simple model was becoming more and more complicated, because the fundamental idea of the circle had to be preserved. It took a mind as brilliant as Kepler's to solve the problem. He substituted elliptical orbits for circular orbits, and everything was explained: all the movements of the planets were accounted for.

Controversially, Jocelyn Bell was excluded from the 1974 Nobel Prize for Physics. She identified the first pulsar signal, in just a few centimetres of the 122 m of chart recording paper – a needle in a haystack discovery – and she identified the second, third and fourth pulsar signals too. It has often been said that genius is the infinite capacity for taking pains, and Jocelyn Bell certainly displayed this quality in her research work.

It seems incredible that she was overlooked by the Nobel Prize adjudicators, and there was widespread consternation among scientists at the time. But Jocelyn Bell Burnell has been philosophical about it. 'In those days, it was believed that science was done, driven by, great men … And that these men had a fleet of minions under them who did their every bidding and did not think. It also came at the stage where I had a small child and I was struggling with how to find proper child-minding, combine a career, and before it was acceptable for women to work. And … it said to me, "Well, men win prizes and young women look after babies." '

Brilliance is not always properly rewarded. But Jocelyn Bell is not at all bitter about the way she was treated in the 1970s. To her it is more important that the scientific community generally has understood and appreciated her contribution to science. She was awarded the DBE, became President of the Royal Astronomical Society, Visiting Professor at the Department of Astrophysics at Oxford, and the first female President of the Institute of Physics.

"You can actually do extremely well out of not getting a Nobel Prize."

IRVING BERLIN

There's No Business Like Show Business

QUOTE ━━

"My ambition is to reach the heart of the average American, not the highbrow nor the lowbrow but that vast intermediate crew which is the real soul of the country. My public is the real people."

BIOGRAPHY ━━━━━━━━━━━━━━━━━━━━━━━━━━━━━━━━━━━━━

NAME: Israel Isidore Baline

BORN: May 11, 1888
Mogilyov, Belarus,
Russian Empire

DIED: September 22, 1989 (Aged 101)
New York City, New York,
United States

NATIONALITY: American

OCCUPATION: Songwriter, composer,
lyricist

The career of the songwriter Irving Berlin is a classic all-American success story. His real name was Israel Baline, and he was born in 1888, far from America, in the village of Tyumun near Mogilyov, Russian Empire (present-day Belarus). It has often been said that America's success as a nation, as a culture, is built on its extraordinary mix of migrant talents. In 1893, his Belarusian-Jewish family emigrated to escape persecution and, at the age of four, the young Israel Baline arrived in America. As so often happened with migrants with foreign names, he adopted a name that would be easier for other Americans to spell and pronounce – Irving Berlin.

He left home at the age of 14 to earn his living, working as a singing waiter in various Chinatown and Bowery cafés, beer halls and cabarets in New York. Then he was noticed by Harry von Tilzer, who hired him to sing von Tilzer songs at Tony Pastor's Music Hall, which had opened in 1881 and is credited with being the birthplace of vaudeville. One of the acts that Irving Berlin was assigned to there was The Three Keatons, one of whom became the great film comedian, Buster Keaton. At Pelham's Café from 1906, he became very popular with customers for his parodies of current popular songs. His talent for improvising new lyrics was mentioned in the press. The waiters at a rival café produced an Italian song, and so Pelham's asked their pianist Nick Nicholson to write a rival song. With his known facility with lyrics, Berlin was asked to write the lyrics. This became *Marie From Sunny Italy*.

Almost by chance, in 1908, Berlin found himself writing the music as well as the words for a second song, *Dorando*. He tried to sell the lyrics on their own to Ted Snyder, but Snyder assumed he had the music as well and offered him $25 for the complete song so, to get the money, Berlin had to supply the music. He sang his melody to an arranger and the arranger fleshed out the accompaniment for him. He used the same technique and the same arranger for another song that year, *The Best of Friends Must Part*. In fact, Berlin never did leave arrangers behind; he was dependent on them for the rest of his career. For the next three years, Berlin honed his skills as a lyricist and found many composers who wanted to work with him.

Irving Berlin never credited his arrangers. He never got beyond creating the melody, which he was able to find on the black notes on the piano, so initially all his tunes were in the key of F sharp. It was the arranger who transposed the tunes into other keys for him. There are photos of Berlin sitting at the piano, but his hands are clearly not playing anything, just hovering over the keys. He listened carefully to the draft arrangements and insisted on change after change until the chord sequence was what he wanted. In a sense, Irving Berlin 'played' his arrangers.

It was unusual to claim credit for both words and music; usually the task of songwriting is divided, with the words written by one person and the music by another. It was perhaps an indication of his flair for publicity rather than mere vanity, when he claimed credit for both.

Soon he was introducing some of his own songs in his performing routine, such as *Alexander's Ragtime Band* and *Everybody's Doin' It*, both written in 1911. These won him instant and international recognition as a songwriter and pioneer of ragtime music. It is another indication of his remarkable skill as a songwriter that his songs were 'number one hits' from the very beginning – his was not a career that was a long gradual haul towards eventual recognition. Everyone could hear that he was a genius from the start.

The evolution of ragtime into jazz owes a lot to Berlin's own innovations. He introduced more complex rhythms and more intricate and inventive melodic lines in songs like *Everybody Step*, written in 1921, and

Pack Up Your Sins in 1922. The increasing popularity of his songs enabled him to open his own music publishing business in 1919. Irving Berlin mounted a 'soldier show' in 1918 and this led on naturally to musical comedy and films in the 1920s and 1930s.

> *"The toughest thing about success is that you've got to keep on being a success."*

Berlin was very soon writing music that seemed to have a truly universal appeal. He left ragtime and jazz behind, finding instead – or indeed creating – an idiom that belonged to Western mid-culture and occupied the middle of the world's sound stage. His songs were emotionally direct yet musically sophisticated. Most popular songs have an opening melody, the main tune, followed by a middle section which may contrast by, for example, being quieter and more thoughtful; then the opening melody is repeated: the A-B-A form. Berlin had a peculiar gift for writing a middle section that was a genuine development section, and therefore musically satisfying.

The harmonies too were often rich and adventurous, whereas run-of-the-mill popular songs often leant on just three or four chords. He was writing songs such as *Always, All Alone, Remember. A Pretty Girl is Like a Melody* uses 22 different chords and *What'll I Do?* a similar number; this is popular music of unusual richness.

By the 1940s, Irving Berlin was at the peak of his career. He wrote music for the hit musicals *Annie Get Your Gun* in 1946 and *Call Me Madam* in 1950. He wrote *Anything You Can Do, There's No Business Like Show Business, Doin' What Comes Naturally, We're a Couple of Swells* and *White Christmas*. In 1939 he wrote *God Bless America*, which became an unofficial second national anthem. In spite of their musical sophistication and their cleverness with words, these are all songs that are incredibly fresh and gutsy, making the most direct emotional pitch imaginable at the audience. It is very hard to believe, listening to them, that he wrote for the money, not for the music.

In 1954, Irving Berlin was awarded a special citation from the President of the United States as a composer of patriotic songs; it was becoming a problem to know how to pay tribute or reward a writer of his brilliance. He had become 'The Nation's Songwriter'. Irving Berlin retired from show business in 1962 at the age of 74. After that, in a long retirement, he led a reclusive life in Manhattan, dying there in 1989 aged over 100.

Berlin's versatility and fluency were remarkable. Most song composers depend on a lyricist to write their words for them. Irving Berlin was able to write the melodies as well as the words, and with equal panache – a very rare accomplishment. In a very long and uniformly successful career, he wrote the words and tunes for over 900 songs.

He seemed to be able to produce an endless stream of likable and instantly memorable songs – songs that are still sung all round the world and remain at the centre of mainstream modern culture. Irving Berlin not only wrote many of the hit songs of the first half of the 20th century, but set the standard for popular songwriting in the West for the rest of the century.

> **"Never hate a song that's sold a half million copies."**

Irving Berlin and the stars of the film,
Alexander's Ragtime Band, 1938.

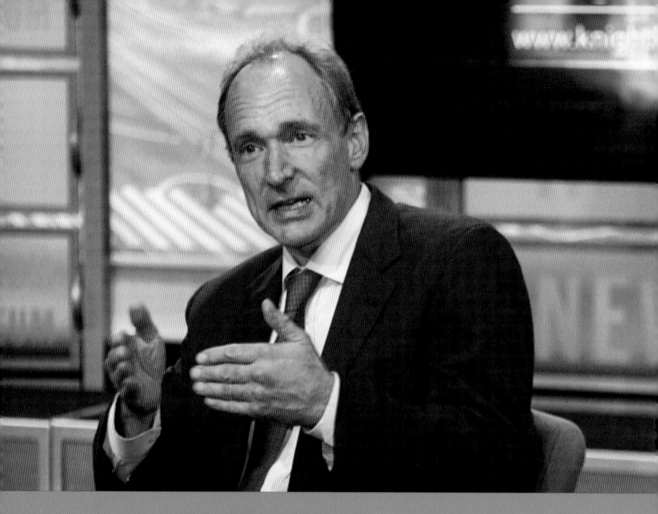

TIM BERNERS-LEE

Weaving the World Wide Web

QUOTE

"When I invented the web, I didn't have to ask anyone's permission."

BIOGRAPHY

NAME: Timothy John Berners-Lee

BORN: June 8, 1955
London, England,
United Kingdom

NATIONALITY: British

OCCUPATION: Computer Scientist,
Director of the World
Wide Web Consortium

The computer scientist Sir Tim Berners-Lee, also known as TimBL, was born in London in 1955. His parents, Conway Berners-Lee and Mary Lee Woods, were computer pioneers: they worked on the first commercially-built computer, the Ferranti Mark 1. Tim Berners-Lee was educated at Emanuel School, London, and Queen's College, Oxford, where he earned a first-class degree in Physics in 1976.

Berners-Lee worked for Plessey Telecommunications Ltd as a software engineer for two years, then as an industrial consultant to D. G. Nash Ltd for a further two years. It was while he was a software consultant, an independent contractor at CERN from June to December 1980, that he proposed and designed a prototype program which he called Enquire. This was a program based on hypertext, and it was designed to facilitate sharing and updating information among researchers. This modest-sounding and very discreet innovation was the forerunner of the World Wide Web.

He then became the founding director responsible for technical design at Image Computer Systems Ltd (1981–84). Then for 10 years he worked at CERN in Geneva; this was the largest Internet node in Europe, and Berners-Lee saw an opportunity to connect hypertext with the Internet. From March 1989 onwards he worked on his highly ambitious global hypertext project, which became known as the World Wide Web in 1990, and became available on the internet from 1991. In his own words, 'I just had to take the hypertext idea and connect it to the Transmission Control Protocol and domain name system ideas and – ta-da! – the World Wide Web … Creating the Web was really an act of desperation, because the situation without it was very difficult when I was working at CERN. Most of the technology involved in the Web, like the hypertext, like the Internet, multifont text objects, had all been designed already. I just had to put them together. It was a step of generalizing, going to a higher level of abstraction, thinking about all the documentation systems out there as being possibly part of a larger imaginary documentation system.'

It was on Christmas Day in 1990, with the help of Robert Cailliau and a young student at CERN, that he achieved the first successful communication between a Hypertext Transfer Protocol client and server by way of the Internet. This was the landmark moment, the Eureka moment. In 1995, Robert Cailliau reminisced about that time. 'During some sessions in the CERN cafeteria, Tim and I tried to find a catchy name for the system. I was determined that the name should not yet again be taken from Greek mythology. Tim proposed "World Wide Web". I liked this very much except that it is difficult to pronounce in French!'

Tim Berners-Lee joined the Laboratory for Computer Science at the Massachusetts Institute of Technology in 1994.

"I basically wrote the code, the specs and documentation for how the client and server talked to each other."

It is no exaggeration to say that the World Wide Web is the greatest invention of our age, and the biggest advance in communications since the invention of television. It is an easy, point-and-click way of navigating and sorting the data stored on the internet. It has turned the information stored on the internet into a colossal, but very accessible, magazine. Addresses on the World Wide Web are instantly recognizable by their opening formula – www for World Wide Web. The web has proved to be such an easy, cheap and flexible platform for communication that it has sparked an explosion of publishing, both professional and amateur. As a result of its popularity, it contains a colossal amount of information and spans a huge range of topics. The lack of editorial control is both its strength and its weakness. The web is all-inclusive, a noisy, babbling marketplace where the mad, the wicked and the ignorant take their place beside the sane, the virtuous and the well-informed.

As if devising the World Wide Web was not a great enough achievement, Tim Berners-Lee designed the URL (universal resource locator) that we are all familiar with – the web address. He also invented HTML, the hypertext markup language. But Berners-Lee has done far more than devise a sophisticated communications system. He has worked hard to keep that system politically neutral, value-neutral, incorrupt and uncontrolled by governments. He directs the World Wide Web Consortium to oversee the Web's continuing development. He holds the 3Com Founders Chair at the MIT Computer Science and Artificial Intelligence Laboratory (CSAIL) and is a director of the Web Science Research Initiative (WSRI), among other positions. In 2009, he launched the World Wide Web Foundation to 'advance the Web to empower humanity by launching transformative programs that build local capacity to leverage the Web as a medium for positive change'.

He has been one of the pioneer voices favouring net neutrality. He believes that internet service providers should supply 'connectivity with no strings attached'; he believes the providers should neither control nor monitor their customers' browsing activities without their express consent. He sees net neutrality as a kind of human network right; 'Threats to the Internet, such as companies or governments that interfere with or snoop on Internet traffic, compromise basic human network rights.'

Thanks to Tim Berners-Lee, we have a global communications system that is open to all. He made his idea freely available; he took out no patent; he takes no royalties. It was an incredibly generous gesture – a great gift to the world. The royalty-free technology was and still is available to be adopted by anyone. Unlike some other benefactors in history, his creativity, originality and generosity have been widely recognized and rewarded. He has been awarded fellowships of the American Academy of Arts and Sciences and the British Royal Society. Several universities, including Harvard, have awarded him honorary doctorates. He was knighted in 2004 and awarded the Order of Merit in 2007. His brilliance lies in seeing the possibilities of existing technologies and systems; he modestly says, 'I just had to put them together.'

"Data is a precious thing and will last longer than the systems themselves."

NIELS BOHR

Quantum Physics and Atomic Ethics

QUOTE ━━━━━━━━━━━━━━━━━━━━━━━━━━━━━━━━━━━━

"An expert is a man who has made all the mistakes which can be made, in a narrow field."

BIOGRAPHY ━━━━━━━━━━━━━━━━━━━━━━━━━━━━━━━━━

NAME: Niels Henrik David Bohr

BORN: October 7, 1885
Copenhagen, Denmark

DIED: November 18, 1962 (Aged 77)
Copenhagen, Denmark

NATIONALITY: Danish

OCCUPATION: Physicist, philosopher

Niels Bohr was born in Copenhagen in 1885. His mother came from a wealthy Jewish banking family and his father was Professor of Physiology at Copenhagen University. Niels and his brother were passionate footballers, and played for the Akademisk-Boldklub: Niels was goalkeeper. He went to university in 1903, studying philosophy and mathematics. Lured by a gold medal competition, he undertook experiments on the properties of surface tension; winning the prize prompted him to switch from philosophy to physics. After graduating, he went on to earn a doctorate in 1911.

Bohr conducted experiments under J. J. Thomson at the Cavendish Laboratory and met and joined Ernest Rutherford at Manchester University, England. Working with the older physicist for four years was a fruitful experience for Bohr, but in 1916 he returned permanently to Copenhagen, where he was given the Chair of Theoretical Physics, a post created specially for him. Then he worked towards establishing a University Institute of Theoretical Physics in 1921, of which he became director.

In 1922, Bohr was awarded the Nobel Prize for Physics for his 'investigation of the structure of atoms and of the radiation emanating from them'. This was in recognition of his early pioneering work in the new field of quantum mechanics. As early as his Manchester days, Bohr had adapted Rutherford's ideas on nuclear structure to harmonize with Planck's quantum theory. The result was a model of atomic structure that is essentially the one that scientists still lean on today. Bohr published his model of atomic structure in 1913. This included the new ideas that electrons travel in orbits round the nucleus of the atom and that the chemical properties of an element are determined by the number of electrons in the outer orbits of its atoms. Another new idea was that an electron could drop from a higher-energy orbit to a lower one, giving off a photon (a light quantum) of energy as it does so. This became one of the bases for quantum theory.

These startling new ideas gave Bohr a leading role in the scientific community, and he came to play a major role in convening lectures and discussion groups. He also became a mentor and adviser for other physicists. Bohr's Institute became an important focus for research into quantum mechanics through the 1920s and 1930s. Bohr was more than a great original scientist, he was a great host and chairman, and a friend and support to other physicists, who appreciated his personal qualities. Often he was in debate with Einstein, but there were few leading physicists of the time who did not have discussions with Bohr.

Niels Bohr devised the original idea that a phenomenon could be analyzed in different ways, separately, because it had several contradictory properties. Physicists have carried out experiments on light that sometimes show light behaving as a stream of particles and sometimes show it behaving as a wave – depending on the design of the experiment. Can light be both? The experiments suggest that this might be so.

Bohr's principle of complementarity allows that this sort of contradiction can exist. In this, as in other areas, Bohr's theories seem to take us into some strange places. The universe is much more complex, much more puzzling, much harder to understand than we could ever have thought possible. Einstein, also a revolutionary thinker, far preferred to think in the deterministic terms of 'classical' physics than in Bohr's new quantum physics, which dealt in probabilities, not certainties. The philosophical issues that arose from this difference of view were widely discussed. Einstein and Bohr had many discussions about these issues, always on friendly terms.

"We are all agreed that your theory is crazy. The question that divides us is whether it is crazy enough to have a chance of being correct."

[Niels Bohr to Wolfgang Pauli]

In 1941, after the German invasion of Denmark during World War II, Werner Heisenberg, who had previously worked as one of Bohr's assistants, met with Bohr in Copenhagen. Heisenberg was now head of the German nuclear energy project and his visit may have been an attempt to enlist Bohr as an intermediary between Germany and Britain. Bohr was one of the very few people in the world who understood what the detonation of a nuclear weapon would be like – he knew, before Hiroshima – and he felt the burden of this knowledge acutely. Whatever happened at this strange meeting, the Germans did not get what they wanted.

In 1943, he heard that he was about to be arrested by the German police, and escaped via Sweden to Britain. There he was introduced to the US secret atomic bomb project, before being taken to the Manhattan Project headquarters at Los Alamos in New Mexico. His involvement in the Manhattan Project was, as far as the American authorities were concerned, to act as a scientific consultant. But he was more concerned about the ethical problems associated with atomic weapons and the prospect of a nuclear arms race; 'That is why I went to America. They didn't need my help in making the atom bomb.' He believed the secrets of atomic weapons should be shared among scientists.

He persuaded Robert Oppenheimer that the atom bomb should in particular be shared with America's allies, the Russians, in the hope of speeding progress. Oppenheimer suggested that Bohr should meet President Franklin D. Roosevelt, to persuade him too. This meeting took place on August 26, 1944. Roosevelt did not agree with Bohr, perhaps because he understood far better than Bohr the true nature of Stalin. Bohr also met Churchill, but Churchill agreed with Roosevelt; he would not trust the Russians with the secrets of atomic weapons. In fact Churchill thought Bohr was dangerous; 'It seems to me Bohr ought to be confined or at any rate made to see that he is very near the edge of mortal crimes,' said Churchill.

After World War II ended, with the explosion of two of the terrible new weapons, Bohr went back to Copenhagen, where he continued to argue for the peaceful use of nuclear energy. When the Danish government awarded him the Order of the Elephant and the right to arms, Bohr adopted the motto 'Opposites are complementary'.

Bohr's brilliance lay in the sheer originality of his ideas, many of them profoundly perplexing. But Niels Bohr was no ivory-tower scholar. He was very active in bringing scientists together to discuss new ideas. He was less concerned with the science of atomic energy, much more concerned with the awfulness of its use to make devastating weapons of war.

When Hitler's persecution of Jews began, Bohr worked actively to help Jewish scientists escape from Germany, offering them a staging-post in Copenhagen while they looked for a permanent home elsewhere. When Bohr was on the run from Hitler, and had to escape to Sweden, he did not save himself immediately by continuing to Britain, as his minders had planned. Instead, he lingered in Sweden, persuading the Swedish King to make a public declaration that Sweden was ready to offer asylum to Jewish refugees. This was broadcast on radio and there was an immediate mass rescue of Danish Jews. During his flight from Stockholm to Britain, in a forgetful professor moment, Bohr forgot to wear his oxygen mask, lapsed into unconsciousness and very nearly died. He commented after the flight, 'I slept like a baby!'

"Prediction is very difficult, especially if it's about the future."

JORGE LUIS BORGES

A Vision of Books and Blindness

QUOTE

"I am not sure that I exist, actually. I am all the writers that I have read, all the people that I have met, all the women that I have loved; all the cities I have visited."

BIOGRAPHY

NAME: Jorge Francisco Isidoro Luis Borges Acevedo

BORN: August 24, 1899
Buenos Aires, Argentina

DIED: June 14, 1986 (Aged 86)
Geneva, Switzerland

NATIONALITY: Argentine

OCCUPATION: Writer, poet, critic, essayist, translator, librarian

The writer Jorge Luis Borges was born into an educated middle-class family who lived in a large house in a poor suburb of Buenos Aires in Argentina. Borges' father, Jorge Guillermo Borges Haslam was of Spanish, Portuguese and English extraction. England and Englishness pervaded Borges' boyhood. At home, there was a library of a thousand English books, which proved to be a shaping influence on his bilingual life. At the age of 11, he was reading Shakespeare in English; at nine he had translated Oscar Wilde's *The Happy Prince* into Spanish, but it seemed so unlikely that his friends assumed that his father was the true translator. This had a certain irony, as Borges' father wanted to be a writer but failed.

In 1914, the family moved to Europe, so that Borges' father could have eye surgery in Geneva. In 1917, Borges met Maurice Abramowicz; it was the start of a life-long literary friendship. Unrest in Argentina persuaded the Borges family to remain in Europe. As World War I ended, they moved from one European city to another: Lugano, Barcelona, Seville and Madrid. Borges read European and American literature voraciously – and wrote. He published his first poem, *Hymn to the Sea*; it was in the style of Walt Whitman.

Borges arrived back in Buenos Aires in 1921 without friends or qualifications, but with a philosophy and a clear idea of what and how he wanted to write. His surreal poems and essays started appearing in literary journals and his first collection of poems appeared in 1923. He co-founded the journals called *Prisma* and *Proa*. Later, he regretted what he had written and tried to call in and destroy surviving copies. In the 1930s, he started exploring existential questions, writing in a style that has been described as 'irreality'. Other Latin American writers of the time were exploring similar themes, influenced by Heidegger and Jean-Paul Sartre. In 1931 the journal *Sur* was founded, and Borges became a regular contributor. He edited a newspaper literary supplement, wrote weekly columns and in 1938 got a job as a library assistant. There was so little work to do at the library that it only took an hour a day; the rest of the time he spent in the library basement, writing.

"I have always imagined that Paradise will be a kind of library."

The year 1938 was life-changing. His father, to whom he was very close, died. Then Borges himself sustained a serious head injury. When recovering, he experimented with a new way of writing, the style for which he became famous. The first story in his new style was *Pierre Menard, Author of The Quixote*, which explored father-son relationships and the nature of authorship, which became central issues in his life. The title story in a 1941 collection called *The Garden of Forking Paths* is a combination of book and maze; it can be read in many ways. With it Borges invented the hypertext novel and went on to describe a universe based on the structure of such a book. *The Garden of Forking Paths* was well-received, but it did not win the accolades his admirers expected. His supporters published a lengthy collection of tributes in *Reparation for Borges*.

Borges' eyesight – though not his vision – began to deteriorate in his early thirties, and he began a new career as a public lecturer. It was this role that made him into a public figure. He became President of the Argentine Society of Writers. One of his short stories, *Emma Zunz*, was made into a film called *Days of Hate* in 1954, and Borges started writing screenplays. By the late 1950s, he was completely blind. In 1955, he was offered the directorship of the Argentine National Library, and he was acutely aware of the irony of this moment.

No-one should see tears or reproach in this declaration of the majesty of God; who with magnificent irony gives me books and blindness at one touch.

Borges was awarded Argentina's National Prize for Literature, and the first of many honorary doctorates. Borges' stories and poems were published in English translations during the 1950s, but his international fame dates from the early 1960s, marked by the award of the first Prix International, which he shared with Samuel Beckett. Many other awards followed, including the French *Legion d'Honneur* in 1983.

As his eyesight worsened, Borges relied increasingly on his mother. When he could not read or write any more, his mother became his secretary and amanuensis. In 1967, when his mother reached the age of 90, Borges married Elsa Millán, and his friends believed that the marriage had been arranged by his mother as she anticipated her death. But the substitute carer lasted only three years. After separating from Elsa, Borges moved back in with his mother. As his eyesight deteriorated, he wrote more poems, because their shortness meant that while he was composing he could carry the full text in his head, until it was ready for someone to write down for him. Jorge Luis Borges died of liver cancer in Geneva in 1986.

His political commitment was intense. He was a great admirer of German literature. In the 1930s and 40s he published several essays attacking Nazism and its racist ideology; he was particularly incensed by German anti-semitism. He saw what was happening in Germany, including its rewriting of history, as a 'chaotic descent into darkness'. He was to suffer for these views when Juan Perón came to power in Argentina in 1946. All ideological critics were dismissed from government posts, and Borges was told he was being 'promoted' from his position at the library to a post as inspector of poultry at Buenos Aires market.

Borges resigned and would never forget or forgive the insult. The way Borges was treated by Perón became a *cause célèbre*; the Argentine Society of Writers held a formal dinner in tribute to him. The speech Borges wrote for the occasion included the comment, 'Dictatorships breed cruelty; more loathsome still is the fact that they breed idiocy.' He went on to make a stand against the Perón regime, and when Perón was driven into exile in September 1955, Borges joined the crowds in the streets, shouting, 'Viva la Patria!' until he was hoarse.

Borges was an extremely talented writer, producing works of incredible range and originality. *The Garden of Forking Paths* led to the coining of the word 'Borgesian' for the quality of non-linearity in story-telling. He is regarded by some as the most important Spanish-language writer since Cervantes. He had enormous influence on other people, and this was only partly to do with his writing. He also had a rare instinct for publicity, for being right at the centre of things. His blindness and his lone-ness in the midst of celebrity also made him a more vulnerable and sympathetic figure.

He was never awarded the Nobel Prize for Literature, possibly because he made the mistake of accepting an award from Chile's General Pinochet. But it continually distressed him – he wanted that prize. In characteristically surreal style, Borges commented, 'Not granting me the Nobel Prize has become a Scandinavian tradition; since I was born they have not been granting it to me.' But prizes are often not awarded fairly, and many other talented people have been overlooked. It is the way things are. And perhaps the fact that he so desperately wanted the Nobel Prize makes Borges a little more ordinary, a little more recognizably like the rest of humanity.

"Poetry remembers that it was an oral art before it was a written art."

NOAM CHOMSKY

Challenging the Structure of Language

QUOTE

"If we don't believe in freedom of expression for people we despise, we don't believe in it at all."

BIOGRAPHY

NAME: Avram Noam Chomsky

BORN: December 7, 1928
Philadelphia, Pennsylvania,
United States

NATIONALITY: American

OCCUPATION: Linguist, philosopher,
cognitive scientist,
logician, political critic,
activist

The linguistics scholar and philosopher, Noam Chomsky, was born into a wealthy Jewish family living in Philadelphia. His father was William Chomsky, a Professor of Hebrew from Ukraine, while his mother, Elsie, grew up in America. Chomsky's parents' first language was Yiddish, but it was taboo within the family to speak it; instead Chomsky's parents brought him up immersed in Hebrew culture and literature. Chomsky was strongly influenced by his uncle, whose news-stand became an 'intellectual centre where professors of this and that argued all night'. Chomsky was also shaped by belonging to a Zionist organization and by frequenting anarchist bookstores.

Noam Chomsky always felt he grew up in a cultural ghetto, feeling threatened by German and Irish Catholics and, in the mid-1930s, by anti-semitism. As a boy he was frightened of Catholics. He said, 'They're the people who beat you up on your way to school … Childhood memories took a long time to overcome.' At 10 years old, Chomsky wrote his first article, about the spread of fascism. By the time he was 12, he was identifying with anarchist politics.

After attending Philadelphia's Central High School, he studied philosophy and linguistics at the University of Pennsylvania. Chomsky was awarded a BA in 1949 and an MA in 1951. In 1949 he married Carol Schatz, and remained married to her until she died in 2008. They went to work for a time in a kibbutz in Israel, which Chomsky loved, except that he 'couldn't stand the ideological atmosphere' of the 1950s, when many left-wing kibbutz members painted too rosy a picture of Stalin's Soviet Union. He liked the communal life of the kibbutz, with children living together, but separately from their parents; it came close to his anarchist ideal.

In 1955, Chomsky gained his PhD in linguistics, elaborating his ideas on language in his 1957 book *Syntactic Structures*. He joined the staff of Massachusetts Institute of Technology (MIT), Cambridge, MA, in 1955. He held the Chair of Modern Languages and Linguistics, 1966–76 and in 1976 was appointed Institute Professor. By the year 2010, Chomsky had taught at MIT continuously for 55 years, while acquiring more than 30 honorary degrees from universities around the world.

Chomsky was politically committed, in 1967 becoming a leading opponent of the Vietnam War. He wrote critical newspaper articles and the 1969 book *American Power and the New Mandarins* established him as a leading figure of American dissent. He has repeatedly criticized US foreign policy and challenged the legitimacy of American power. This has made him a controversial figure, frequently asked by journalists for his views. Perhaps inevitably, because of the polarization of views about US foreign policy, Chomsky has received threats to his life. Chomsky's politics have their roots in the Enlightenment, though he has described himself as an anarchist.

"If you don't like what someone has to say, argue with them."

Chomsky's approach to language challenges structural linguistics, introducing instead transformational grammar. This takes sequences of written or spoken words (utterances) to have a syntax with a formal grammar. His most enduring contribution has been the idea that acquiring knowledge of language using a formal grammar accounts for the creativity of language. Using a formal grammar of a language explains how a speaker or hearer may produce or interpret an infinite number of utterances, including completely novel ones. Many of Chomsky's ideas have, reasonably enough, been misunderstood.

He did not prove that language is entirely

innate, nor did he (quite) discover a universal grammar. What he said was that a baby and a kitten are both capable of inductive reasoning but, if they are exposed to the same linguistic data, the child will eventually understand it and produce language, but the cat will do neither. Whatever the capacity is that people have and cats don't, Chomsky labelled it the language acquisition device (LAD), and he proposed that students of linguistics should try to establish what the LAD is and how it constrains the development of languages. The common features that those constraints would yield are often described as universal grammar (UG).

Chomsky's strongest argument in support of UG is that children acquire language in a surprisingly short time, in spite of having to learn vocabulary; this implies an innate structure is being brought into play. Chomsky makes powerful claims regarding UG. He believes that grammatical principles underpinning languages are innate and fixed.

Difference among languages can be defined in terms of parameter settings in the brain, such as the pro-drop parameter, which indicates whether an explicit subject is always required, as it is in the English language, or can be dropped, as in Spanish. These parameters are compared with switches.

Given this view of language structure, a child who is learning a language only has to have the necessary vocabulary and idioms and to determine the appropriate parameter settings, and those can be done by providing a few examples. This is Chomsky's Principles and Parameters approach, dating from about 1980.

Noam Chomsky's ideas had a strong influence on those researching language acquisition among children, though some, such as Michael Tomasello, argue strongly against Chomsky, and advocate alternative theories. A recurring criticism of the approach of Chomsky and his followers is that it is Anglocentric and Eurocentric. Linguists working within this tradition tend to base their claims on a small sample of

(European) languages and sometimes on just one, English. So, Chomsky's approach to language has been represented as a form of linguistic imperialism. This is ironic, in view of Chomsky's stand on what he sees as America's political imperialism, but contradictions and inconsistencies of this kind are an integral part of human nature.

Chomsky views science as a straightforward quest for explanation, not an inventory of facts. He puts a higher value on devising frameworks and hypotheses than on 'discoveries'. He values science, but sees it as inadequate to understand complex human affairs, in which he is deeply interested. 'Science talks about very simple things. As soon as things become too complex, science can't deal with them … Human affairs are way too complicated,' he said.

Chomsky has engaged repeatedly and vigorously in debates on a variety of issues. He has been criticized for having a boring speaking voice, but he characteristically defends this too. "People are interested in the issues, not in eloquence. We should keep emotion out of it." Here we see a brilliant mind that is prepared to travel its own path, and it has gathered a significantly large following – because of its engagement, commitment and seriousness.

He recently dared once more to criticize American foreign policy, on the death of Osama bin Laden. We might disagree with Chomsky or agree with him, but there is no denying the refreshing sharpness of his mind and the courage of his dissidence:

> *"We might ask ourselves how we would be reacting if Iraqi commandos landed at George W. Bush's compound, assassinated him, and dumped his body in the Atlantic. His crimes vastly exceed bin Laden's, and he is not a 'suspect' but the 'decider' who gave the orders."*

JOSEPH CONRAD

The Inextinguishable Fire of Passion

"A word carries far, very far, deals destruction through time as the bullets go flying through space."

BIOGRAPHY

NAME: Józef Teodor Konrad Korzeniowski

BORN: December 3, 1857
Berdichev, Kiev, Ukraine (then part of the Kingdom of Poland)

DIED: August 3, 1924 (Aged 66)
Bishopsbourne, England, United Kingdom

NATIONALITY: Polish-British

OCCUPATION: Novelist, short-story writer

Joseph Conrad was a Polish novelist of great power and distinction, writing four of the '100 Best Novels of the 20th Century' (according to the Random House Modern Library list): *The Secret Agent, Nostromo, Lord Jim* and *Heart of Darkness*. He was born into an aristocratic Polish family in Berdichev, Ukraine. His father, Apollo Korzeniowski, was a playwright who translated Victor Hugo, Dickens and Shakespeare into Polish. After Conrad was orphaned at the age of 11, he was cared for by his uncle in Kraków, Poland. At the age of 16, Conrad travelled to Marseilles to become a seaman. This was a flight from danger, as Conrad had been turned down when he applied for Austro-Hungarian citizenship, leaving him liable to conscription into the Russian Army. But the alternative life he had chosen was itself full of risk and adventure. He dabbled in gun-running and political conspiracy, escapades that later found their way into the novel *The Arrow of Gold*. A voyage along the Colombian coast gave him the material for *Nostromo*.

He signed on for a series of voyages along the east coast of England from Lowestoft to Newcastle upon Tyne. During these voyages of about 200 miles (320 km) each, he learned English – or at least a vivid industrial version of it complete with curses and swear words – from the other crew members. This was to have a major effect on his later writing style.

The coastal voyages were full of incident. In 1881, Conrad sailed for Newcastle as second mate on the *Palestine*, a small ship with a crew of 13. They were sailing to collect coal which they would take all the way to Bangkok, Thailand. But hampered by a gale, it took them 16 days to reach the river Tyne. Once there, the *Palestine* had to wait for a berth, and while waiting was rammed by a steamer. Two months later, the *Palestine* sailed from Newcastle bound for Bangkok, but sprang a leak in the English Channel. They were stuck in Falmouth on the south coast of England for the next nine months. In March 1883, two years after their departure from Newcastle, the ship finally reached Java, Indonesia, where the coal caught fire. The ship was engulfed in flames with the crew precariously reaching shore in open boats. This whole adventurous, eventful voyage gave Conrad the material for his novel, *Youth*.

1886 was a landmark year. Conrad gained his Master Mariner's certificate, his British citizenship and his name; he gave up the name Korzeniowski and adopted Conrad. In 1889, he visited central Africa, becoming the captain of a Congo steamboat. This was to be the central adventure of his life, the defining rite of passage. In the Congo he witnessed terrible atrocities inflicted on the native African people, an experience that informed his most famous and challenging work, *Heart of Darkness*. What he saw crystallized his view of human nature and his beliefs about himself.

Sailing up the Congo described in *Heart of Darkness* closely follows Conrad's own voyage. During this journey into the heart of Africa, he witnessed a profoundly disturbing insight into the nature of evil. In a way he had been led to this point by his series of adventures at sea, where he had experienced isolation, loneliness, corruption and the pitiless hostility of nature. All this found its way into his writing. Springing from his sea-faring experiences was the observation of human failings which also found its way into the fabric of his novels.

Conrad made two voyages to Australia aboard the clipper ship *Torrens* – he stepped down in rank from captain to first mate in order to do so – before retiring from the sea in 1894. While he was aboard the *Torrens* he started writing his first novel, *Almayer's Folly*. He left the sea and began his literary career.

Also in 1896, at the age of 38, he married an English woman, Jessie George, setting up home in a semi-detached house in Stanford-le-Hope in Essex, England.

His socio-political position looked backwards to his aristocratic origins. He was patronizing towards ordinary people and the slums in which they lived. He detested notions of equality, yet he was deeply disturbed by the inhumane way in which people treated each other and the consequences of that inhumanity. He had no taste for democracy, yet his work burns with a detestation of cruelty – a liberal impulse. He was a man of many contradictions.

Almayer's Folly (1895) and its successor, *An Outcast of the Islands* (1896), laid the foundation of Conrad's reputation as a teller of romantic exotic tales. But this was a fundamental misunderstanding of his purpose as a writer that he found frustrating. Although his ability as a writer was appreciated by the intellectual elite, Conrad seemed unable to achieve financial success. He became subject to bouts of depression, pessimism and self-doubt. It was only with the publication of *Chance* in 1913 that he became a popular author in a wider market. From then on, his literary status and his wealth grew. He declined a knighthood offered in 1924 and almost immediately afterwards died of a heart attack.

> *"Words, as is well known, are the great foes of reality."*

Conrad's work is characterized by his key personality traits, doubt, pessimism about human nature, and relentless moral judgement. His sense of personal isolation is projected into his books by placing the characters in remote, confined settings, on board a lonely vessel on a far flung sea or in a distant country village. He wrote a prose that is very close to poetry. In his impassioned preface to *The Nigger of the Narcissus* (1897) he wrote that as an artist he was trying:

> *by the power of the written word to make you hear, to make you feel … before all, to make you see. That – and no more, and it is everything. If I succeed, you shall find … that glimpse of truth for which you have forgotten to ask.*

In the first half of the 20th century, Conrad was the English novelist with the most consistent command of atmosphere and precision of language. His command of English was all the more remarkable as English was his *third* language. There is a unique weight in his writing that springs from the use of devices such as triple parallelism – 'all that mysterious life of the wilderness that stirs in the forest, in the jungles, in the hearts of wild men'. There is also a grandeur that comes from rhetorical abstraction – 'the stillness of an implacable force brooding over an inscrutable intention'. Conrad made friends easily, and his circle included other great writers such as Stephen Crane and Henry James. One of his friends, T. E. Lawrence, commented, 'He's absolutely the most haunting thing in prose that ever was: I wish I knew how every paragraph he writes goes on sounding in waves, like the note of a tenor bell, after it stops.'

Some contemporary critics commented that his pessimism was off-putting. But the unfolding events of the early 20th century showed that Conrad's pessimism was justified, and admiration for his work grew and grew. Critics of Conrad's portrayal of black people in *Heart of Darkness* have misunderstood what Conrad is doing. The racist depiction of the Africans is in the heart of the protagonists, not in Conrad's heart: in a mixture of sarcasm and creative empathy, Conrad is showing the reader how the inhumane exploiters and tormentors of Africans see their victims – 'that glimpse of truth for which you have forgotten to ask'. It does not make easy reading, and Conrad's greatness is still not universally appreciated.

FRANCIS CRICK

Discovering the Secret of Life

QUOTE

"It seems likely that most if not all the genetic information in any organism is carried by nucleic acid – usually by DNA."

BIOGRAPHY

NAME: Francis Harry Compton Crick

BORN: June 8, 1916
Northampton, England,
United Kingdom

DIED: July 28, 2004 (Aged 88)
San Diego, California,
United States

NATIONALITY: British

OCCUPATION: Molecular biologist,
biophysicist, neuroscientist

Francis Crick, the molecular biologist and co-discoverer of the molecular structure of DNA, was born and brought up in Northampton, where his father ran a shoe factory. Crick was awarded a BSc in physics in 1937 at University College, London. He started a PhD research project but this was interrupted by the outbreak of war in 1939. During World War II he worked as a scientist for the British Admiralty, principally on magnetic and acoustic mines. In 1947, Crick left the Admiralty to study biology. He was at a disadvantage, because at that time, he knew no biology and practically no organic chemistry or crystallography. But he got a studentship from the Medical Research Council and with some financial support from his family he went to do research work at the Strangeways Research Laboratory at Cambridge.

In 1949 Francis Crick joined the Medical Research Council Unit, remaining a member for the rest of his life. He had to spend a good deal of time filling the gaps in his knowledge, yet in collaboration with others he worked out a general theory of X-ray diffraction by a helix and suggested that the alpha-keratin pattern was created by alpha helices coiled round each other. This was the origin of the idea of the double-helix. As is often the way in science, others (Linus Pauling and R. B. Corey) came to the same conclusion at the same time.

It was not until 1954 that, as a mature student, Crick achieved his doctorate, and by then he had discovered the molecular structure of DNA – though not without considerable input from other scientists.

A major influence on Francis Crick's career was his close working relationship and friendship with James D. Watson, a young American biologist who joined the laboratory in 1951 at the age of 23; Crick was then 35. In 1953, after working closely with Watson for two years, Crick constructed a molecular model of the extremely complex genetic material known as DNA (deoxyribonucleic acid). It had already become clear in the 1940s that a large molecule such as protein was likely to be the bearer of genetic material, but some evidence pointed to another macromolecule, DNA, as a likelier candidate. So Crick's focus on analyzing DNA was with a clear view of unravelling genetic codes.

Francis Crick thought Rosalind Franklin and Maurice Wilkins at King's College, London, had failed to find a molecular model because of a failure in their working relationship; with more collaboration, he believed, they might have achieved it. Crick was confident that it could be done, and eventually got permission to have a second attempt from his supervisor and from Maurice Wilkins.

Crick and Watson used 'Photo 51' as their window on the DNA molecule. This photo was the X-ray diffraction image produced by Raymond Gosling and Rosalind Franklin; it was supplied by Gosling and Franklin's co-worker Maurice Wilkins. Rosalind Franklin was useful to Crick because of her advanced chemistry knowledge, which she shared with him. She had pointed out to Crick and Watson that their first attempt at a double-helix model (in 1951), with the phosphates at the centre, was incorrect.

The second molecular model Crick and Watson extracted from the image of the very complex DNA molecule was also famously in the form of a double helix. Crick and Watson were not supposed to be working on DNA. Crick was writing up his PhD thesis, and Watson had other work too. But Crick made a grab for Rosalind Franklin's results and used them to infer the DNA structure.

Francis Crick was unstoppable by this stage, and determined to get the model published before a likely American rival, Linus Pauling, got there first. The political situation was almost as complicated as the molecule. Pauling at that stage had little contact with the English researchers and as it happened was preoccupied with proteins, not DNA, but it was the *perceived* threat from Pauling that made Crick desperate for a result.

> *"There is no scientific study more vital to man than the study of his own brain. Our entire view of the universe depends on it."*

When Crick died in San Diego of colon cancer in 2004, James Watson said, 'I will always remember Francis for his extraordinary focused intelligence. He treated me as though I were a member of his family. I always looked forward to being with him and speaking to him.' Crick was criticized by some fellow-scientists for being talkative to the point of brashness, and lacking in modesty. He talked rapidly, loudly, though with humour and an infectious laugh. One co-worker described him as 'a brainstorming intellectual powerhouse with a mischievous smile. Francis was never mean-spirited, just incisive. He detected microscopic flaws in logic. In a room full of smart scientists, Francis continually re-earned his position as the heavyweight champ.'

Crick was awarded the Nobel Prize for Medicine and Physiology in 1962, jointly with James Watson and Maurice Wilkins. James Watson returned to America, where he became director of the Cold Spring Biological Laboratories in New York.

The discovery of the structure of DNA and its significance was one of the great scientific breakthroughs of the second half of the 20th century. It was a discovery with lots of ramifications. When it emerged that everyone has a different DNA profile, the possibility for using it for identification presented itself and now, DNA has become a major forensic tool. A criminal has to leave only a few traces of human tissue at the scene of a crime, and he or she can be identified. This ground-breaking technique has made it possible to solve crimes committed decades ago (until recently thought unsolvable) and also, disturbingly, prove that some people serving very long prison sentences really did not commit the crimes for which they were convicted. At least DNA has ensured their release, and the possibility that there will be fewer miscarriages of justice in the future.

Family members have related DNA, so DNA analysis can establish kinship links; this was how the rediscovered remains of Tsar Nicholas II and his family were identified. This kinship feature can also help to resolve cases of disputed paternity. Since DNA can survive for a long time after death, it also proves valuable to historians, archaeologists and anthropologists in establishing kinship groups. DNA has opened many doors.

Crick had forced himself to switch from the 'elegance and deep simplicity' of physics to the 'elaborate chemical mechanisms that natural selection had evolved over billions of years'. He had 'to be born again'. Crick admitted that physics had taught him arrogance; seeing that physics was already a success (by implication through arrogance) convinced him that similar great advances should also be possible in other sciences, like biology. He felt that this confident attitude encouraged him to be more daring than most biologists.

The achievement was a brilliant one, but there remains a fundamental ethical question. Was it really right for Francis Crick to have access to Rosalind Franklin's report of 1952 without her permission, without her knowledge even, and before she had had the chance to publish? Her interpretation – not necessarily a helical structure – stood in his way. Franklin's evidence was essential to his case and if he waited Pauling might have beaten him to the finishing line.

Crick declined a CBE in 1963 and later refused a knighthood, but he did accept the Order of Merit in 1991.

> *"How do I know what I think until I hear what I say?"*

MARIE CURIE

The Most Inspirational Woman in Science

QUOTE ━━━━━━━━━━━━━━━━━━━━━━━━━━━━━━━━━━━━━

"Nothing in life is to be feared, it is only to be understood. Now is the time to understand more, so that we may fear less."

BIOGRAPHY ━━━━━━━━━━━━━━━━━━━━━━━━━━━━━━━━━

NAME: Marie Salomea Skłodowska-Curie

BORN: November 7, 1867
Warsaw, Poland

DIED: July 4, 1934 (Aged 66)
Passy, Haute-Savoie, France

NATIONALITY: Polish (by birth), French (by marriage)

OCCUPATION: Physicist, chemist

Marie Curie was born as Maria Skłodowska in 1867 in Warsaw, where she received her early scientific training from her father, a well-known teacher who was the director of two boys' schools. Marie's mother was also a teacher: she ran a prestigious girls' boarding school, but died when Marie was only 12 years old. They gave Marie a supportive but strange upbringing, with her father an atheist and her mother a devout Catholic. The deaths of her mother and one of her sisters caused Marie to have doubts and she moved from Catholicism towards agnosticism.

There was little family money, so Marie agreed with one of her sisters that they would take it in turns to finance one another's further education. So Marie became a governess in order to support her sister Bronislawa's medical studies in Paris. She fell in love with Kazimierz Zorawski, the son of one of the families for whom she was working.

Zorawski's parents refused to allow him to marry the penniless girl – and sacked her. For some time she hoped that the Zorawski family might relent but, when she eventually had a letter from Kazimierz finally ending the relationship, she went to join her sister in Paris; Bronislawa had been urging her to go for some time.

She arrived in Paris in October 1891 and struggled to earn her keep while working for her science degree at the Sorbonne. She graduated in physics in 1893 and started working at an industrial laboratory. She paid for her own mathematics education, and earned her degree in 1894. That year she met Pierre Curie. She had started her science career in Paris with an investigation of the magnetic properties of different kinds of steel. It was, appropriately, magnetism that drew Pierre and Marie together.

She returned for the summer to Warsaw, and this temporary separation from Pierre intensified their feelings for each other. At that point she believed she would return to Poland to work in her research field, but she was refused a place at Kraków University on the grounds that she was a woman, so she returned to Paris and married Pierre. They shared interests in long bicycle rides and foreign travel, and their research was also a shared enthusiasm; Marie had found not only a partner but a reliable scientific collaborator.

Marie Curie worked side-by-side with her husband on magnetism and radioactivity. She invented the word 'radioactivity' in 1898, though it was Henri Becquerel who had actually discovered the phenomenon two years before. Marie was very well aware of the politics of science, and the importance of promptly publishing discoveries so establishing her ownership of the idea. She knew that Becquerel had presented his discovery of radioactivity to the *Académie des Sciences* just in time (the day after he had made it). If he had left it later, credit for the discovery, and the Nobel Prize, would probably have gone to Silvanus Thompson instead.

Marie Curie went for the same swift means of establishing her priority on the discovery, using her former professor to read her paper to the *Académie* for her. When she wrote her biography of her husband, she was similarly careful to underline the fact that it was she who had made some of the discoveries – just in case some scientists suspected that a woman was incapable of such cleverness!

The Curies also isolated two new elements from the mineral pitchblende, radium and polonium, which she named after her native Poland. They went on to explore the properties of radium and its transformation products. The work that Marie Curie and her husband did on radium laid the foundations for much of the later research on nuclear physics and chemistry.

In 1903, Marie and Pierre Curie were

Pierre and Marie Curie in their Paris laboratory around 1900.

jointly awarded the Nobel Prize for Physics, together with Henri Becquerel. The prize was for the discovery of radioactivity. In the same year, Marie submitted the results of her work in a doctorate thesis. It was remarkable achievement, to have been awarded the Nobel Prize before being awarded her doctorate.

> *"I am one of those who think, like Nobel, that humanity will draw more good than evil from new discoveries."*

In 1905, Pierre Curie was elected to the *Académie des Sciences*. The following year, on April 19, he was killed instantly when he was run over by a cart in a Paris street. After her husband's unexpected death, Marie was 'incurably wretched and lonely'. But she was elected to succeed him as Professor of Physics at the Sorbonne. In 1910, she isolated pure radium and was awarded the Nobel Prize for Chemistry in 1911, this time for discovering radium and clarifying its properties. After winning that prize, she collapsed again into depression; she was subject to endless suspicion and gossip in France, because she was both a woman and a foreigner.

After World War I, Marie Curie was made director of the research department of the Radium Institute in Paris, and she continued in this post until 1934. She set up another laboratory in Warsaw and, in 1929, US President Herbert Hoover gave her $50,000 donated by American friends of science, so that she could buy radium to use in her research.

Her elder daughter Irène became a nuclear physicist who shared a Nobel Prize for artificially producing radioactive elements, and after World War II joined the French Atomic Energy Commission. Marie Curie's younger daughter, Ève, became a well-known musician and writer, as well as working for the French resistance in World War II. Marie Curie died in the south of France in July 1934, having unwittingly exposed herself to dangerous doses of radiation during the course of her work. In both senses, she had given her life to science.

She had laid the foundations for research that would lead to the development of nuclear weapons, nuclear power stations and new treatments for cancer. Her research overturned established ideas in both physics and chemistry, and it continues to shape the world in the 21st century.

But her life also had profound and far-reaching effects on Western society. To achieve her extraordinary scientific results, she had to overcome many social and professional barriers because she was a woman. This was as true in France as it was in Poland. Marie Curie was emancipated, independent and ahead of her time. She was the first woman to be awarded a Nobel Prize, and is rightly seen as the precursor of modern feminism. But, she was an example in another important way: she was unspoilt. Einstein commented that she was probably the only person he had met who remained uncorrupted by fame.

But it was not an entirely happy life. She made a brave recovery from losing her first love, Kazimierz Zorawski, by finding Pierre Curie, but slumped into despair, twice, after Pierre's death. A year after her own death, in 1935, a statue of Marie Skłodowska-Curie was erected in Warsaw outside the Radium Institute she had founded in 1932. In later years, an old man, and now a distinguished mathematician, Kazimierz Zorawski would go to gaze at the statue – wondering how life might have been …

> *"Life is not easy for any of us. But what of that? We must have perseverance and above all confidence in ourselves."*

MILES DAVIS

The Supreme Definition of Cool

QUOTE ━━━━━━━━━━━━━━━━━━━━━━━━━━━━━━━━

"Music and life are all about style."

BIOGRAPHY ━━━━━━━━━━━━━━━━━━━━━━━━━━━━

NAME: Miles Dewey Davis III

BORN: May 26, 1926
Alton, Illinois, United States

DIED: September 28, 1991 (Aged 65)
Santa Monica, California,
United States

NATIONALITY: American

OCCUPATION: Jazz musician, trumpeter,
bandleader, composer

The story of the legendary jazz trumpeter Miles Davis is no simple rags-to-riches story. He was born into an affluent African-American family. His father, Dr Miles Henry Davis, was an Illinois dentist who owned a ranch in Arkansas, where the young Miles Dewey Davis learned to ride. Miles' mother was Cleota Mae Henry, a proficient blues pianist who for some reason hid her musical talent from her son.

His mother wanted him to learn to play the piano, but when Miles Davis was 13, his father gave him a trumpet and arranged for him to have lessons with Elwood Buchanan, a local musician. Miles later speculated that his father may have chosen the trumpet for him deliberately to annoy his wife, who hated the sound of the trumpet. The fashion at the time was to use vibrato, but when Miles started using heavy vibrato, Buchanan slapped his knuckles. The clean, pure sound that this produced carried Miles through his musical career and became his signature. He commented, 'I prefer a round sound with no attitude in it, like a round voice with not too much tremolo.'

When he was 17 years old, Miles spent a year playing in Eddie Randle's Band. In 1944, the Billy Eckstine band visited East St Louis. Charlie Parker and Dizzy Gillespie were band members. When Buddy Anderson was off sick for a couple of weeks, Miles was taken on as third trumpet. Suddenly Miles was playing with jazz musicians of the highest order. But, even so, Mr and Mrs Davis still insisted on Miles continuing his education. In the autumn of 1944, after he graduated from high school, Miles went to New York to study at the Juilliard School of Music.

Against advice, he spent a good deal of time trying to track down Charlie Parker. Miles finally found him, and he became one of the group of musicians who played nightly sessions at Harlem nightclubs. Miles dropped out of the Juilliard School, frustrated with its emphasis on European classical music, but he was still ready to acknowledge that Juilliard gave him a useful grounding in music theory and helped him improve his trumpet technique.

Miles Davis started playing professionally in clubs with Coleman Hawkins. A rite of passage was going into a recording studio for the first time, in 1945, with Herbie Fields' group. Dizzy Gillespie parted company from Charlie Parker, and Davis took Gillespie's place in the Charlie Parker Quintet. Relationships became strained because of Parker's drug-induced erratic mood swings and, in December 1948, after Davis complained that he had not been paid, he left the group. This enabled him to freelance, and play with different jazz groups.

An important development was working with the Canadian composer and arranger Gil Evans. There were experiments with a new grouping of nine instruments. Davis was keen to create a sound like the human voice, and use new arrangements to create a relaxed melodic sound in improvisations. The debut performances at the Royal Roost gave a high profile to the arrangers, another new departure: 'Miles Davis Nonet: Arrangements by Gil Evans, John Lewis and Gerry Mulligan.' This sort of innovation had to be negotiated with the club's managers. Using white musicians in the group was seen by some of the black jazz players as a kind of treason, but Davis brushed aside racist criticism. To him it was the music that counted.

> *"Good music is good - no matter what kind of music it is."*

Capitol Records released an album which contained music from several 1949–1950 recording sessions. The record's title was significant – *The Birth of the Cool*. It was a new music, and it became known as 'cool jazz'. Miles knew how important this was, and even turned down the chance of a job with Duke Ellington's orchestra to carry on working on it. The Nonet was a commercial failure. Miles smarted under the criticism and was bitter when, later, white 'cool jazz' musicians like Mulligan and Dave Brubeck made a lot of money from it.

In 1949, Miles went on tour in Paris, where he began a relationship with the French actress and singer Juliette Gréco. Friends tried to persuade him to stay in Paris, where jazz musicians were shown respect, but he decided to return to New York. There he went into a deep depression, partly because of separation from Juliette Gréco, partly because of the lack of critical appreciation of his music; another relationship unravelled at the same time.

This was the low point in his life when Miles started taking heroin. He was not alone among jazz musicians at that time in developing an addiction, but it affected his ability to perform – and addiction was killing some of his friends (Fats Navarro and Freddie Webster). He tried several times to end his addiction, finally succeeding in St Louis in 1954; he stayed away from New York, where drugs were too easily come by.

Eventually the creativity revived; post-recovery he went on making music, and releasing many records. He started using the Harmon mute to play close to the microphone; this created an intimate sound that became his characteristic signature. His phrasing too became looser and more relaxed. The distinctive and unmistakable Miles Davis sound that he had been striving for was fully formed. There was a change in style to 'hard bop', which used slower tempi, simpler, more conventional harmonies, and a harder beat. Often popular tunes and standards from the American songbook were used as starting points. This is music that takes a step back from experimental jazz towards popular music.

"You have to play a long time to be able to play like yourself."

Back in New York, Miles formed a quintet. This was successful but disbanded after a series of quarrels that Davis blamed on the drug problems of the other musicians in the group. The quintet was re-formed as a sextet to record *Milestones*, which anticipated the new directions he expected to take. Then he brought in the brilliant young white pianist Bill Evans.

Miles Davis went on innovating, performing and recording for another 40 years, producing *Tutu* in 1986, which used a range of modern studio acoustic techniques. Half a century after his first releases his music was still being enthusiastically reviewed.

Miles died in 1991, at the age of 65, from complications after a stroke. He was an innovative composer and bandleader, and many jazz performers enhanced their careers by playing in his ensembles. After a string of Grammy awards, he was given a Grammy Lifetime Achievement Award in 1990. Miles Davis was one of the most innovative figures in the history of jazz, playing a central role in every major development from the 1940s to the 1980s. The album *Kind of Blue* sold more copies than any other record in the history of jazz.

"I know what I've done for music, but don't call me a legend. Just call me Miles."

WALT DISNEY

Some Dreams Do Come True

QUOTE

"Laughter is timeless. Imagination has no age. And dreams are forever."

BIOGRAPHY

NAME: Walter Elias Disney

BORN: December 5, 1901
Hermosa, Chicago, Illinois,
United States

DIED: December 15, 1966 (Aged 65)
Burbank, California,
United States

NATIONALITY: American

OCCUPATION: Business magnate,
animator, film producer,
director, screenwriter,
actor

Walt Disney was the son of an Irish-Canadian father and a German-American mother. Walt's father, Elias Disney, worked for a time on a farm at Marceline in Missouri, which is where young Walt first found his love for drawing. He was encouraged in this by a neighbour, Doc Sherwood, who paid him to draw pictures of Rupert, his horse. After four years at Marceline, the Disneys moved to Kansas City, where Walt attended the Benton Grammar School and met Walter Pfeiffer. The Pfeiffer family were theatre lovers; they introduced Walt to the world of vaudeville and motion pictures, and Walt spent more and more time with them.

In 1917, the Disney family moved back to Chicago, where Walt had been born; there Walt started his freshman year at McKinley High School and took evening classes at the Chicago Art Institute. He became the cartoonist for the school newspaper. His subjects were patriotic, with a focus on World War I issues. He dropped out of school in an attempt to join the army, but he was rejected because of his age: he was 16. Then he and a friend decided to join the Red Cross, and he was sent to France for a year to drive an ambulance, though only after the war had ended.

By 1919 he was back in Chicago looking for work. He decided he would be a newspaper artist, drawing political cartoons or comic strips, but no-one wanted to hire him. His brother got him a job at the Pesmen-Rubin Art Studio, where he designed ads for newspapers, magazines and movie theatres. At the art studio he met the cartoonist Ubbe Iwerks, and they decided to set up their own company. Iwerks-Disney Commercial Artists did not last long and the two young men became employees again, at the Kansas City Film Ad Company. There Walt Disney made commercials based on cut-out animation. This was a technique that really interested Disney and he decided to become an animator. The Ad Company's owner generously allowed Disney to borrow a camera to take home and experiment with animation in his own time. Disney was on a programme of self-education. He read Edwin G. Lutz's book *Animated Cartoons: How They Are Made*, and saw that cel animation had more potential for development than the cut-out animation he was doing for the Ad Company.

Walt Disney confidently decided that he would set up his own animation business, recruiting Fred Harman, a co-worker at the Ad Company, as his first employee. Disney and Harman negotiated a deal with Frank L. Newman, the most popular showman in Kansas City, to screen their *Laugh-O-Gram* cartoons at his theatre. Disney's cartoons became popular in the area, popular enough for Disney to acquire a studio, Laugh-O-Gram, and hire a large number of extra animators to take on the increasing work, including his friend Ubbe Iwerks. But Disney was over-reaching, and the Laugh-O-Gram income did not cover the generous salaries he was paying; the company went broke.

Resilient as ever, Disney decided to move to Hollywood, where he set about finding a distributor for his *Alice Comedies*, which he had started making in Kansas. The New York distributor Margaret Winkler was interested in giving him a deal for animated shorts based on *Alice's Wonderland*. Soon the Disney Brothers' Studio was established with his brother Roy.

Iwerks and his family moved to Hollywood to work with Disney. The *Alice Comedies* were fairly successful, but Disney found he was more interested in animated characters, and animals in particular. This led to *Oswald the Lucky Rabbit* (1926), created and drawn by Iwerks: it was a success. A setback was finding that most of his main animators were being 'stolen' by a rival, along with the Oswald character, though Iwerks stayed with Disney.

Walt Disney and Mickey Mouse
statue at Disneyland, California.

Losing Oswald meant that Disney had to come up with a new character. Disney did some initial sketches which Iwerks reworked to make the character easier to animate. Lillian Disney came up with the name, and Mickey Mouse made his film debut in a 1927 silent short cartoon called *Plane Crazy*.

But technology was fast advancing and in 1928, after failing to find distributor interest for the silent Mickey, Disney gave the mouse a voice in his first sound cartoon called *Steamboat Willie*. A businessman named Pat Powers provided Disney with both distribution and the Cinephone, a sound-synchronization process. *Steamboat Willie* became a huge success, and all future Mickey cartoons were released with soundtracks.

By 1932, Mickey Mouse had became the most popular cartoon character in the world and Disney received a special Academy Award for his creation. By 1935, colour animation had arrived at the Disney Studios along with a cast of popular supporting cartoon characters such as Donald Duck, Goofy and Pluto. Disney himself performed the voice of Mickey Mouse until 1947.

> *"I only hope that we don't lose sight of one thing - that it was all started by a mouse."*

Always keen to push the boundaries, Disney had begun plans to produce a full-length colour cartoon movie as early as 1934. When the rest of the US film industry learned of his dream they dubbed the project 'Disney's Folly' and were certain that the project would bankrupt the studio. Enormous numbers of hand-drawn images were required. This mountain of work was shared among a vast team of dedicated artists. Disney was a hard task-master and demanded incredibly high standards from his staff. But eventually, in 1937, after many trials and tribulations, *Snow White and the Seven Dwarfs* was released to massive acclaim. The income from this one cartoon enabled Disney to open new state of the art studios in Burbank, California in 1939, where he went on to make many more feature-length animations during the 1940s, 1950s and 1960s. *Pinocchio, Dumbo, Bambi, Peter Pan, Alice in Wonderland, Lady and the Tramp, One Hundred and One Dalmations, Sleeping Beauty* and *Jungle Book,* all became part of a seemingly endless catalogue of 20th century classics.

Fantasia was a different experiment. Disney took an orchestral score, conducted by Leopold Stokowski, and made an animated cartoon film to synchronize with the music. Many of the effects were surreal. It is an outstanding piece of craftsmanship, but it lacked a storyline and has never had a popular following.

In 1948, Walt Disney embarked on yet another new venture, a series of documentary nature films, which included *The Living Desert,* made in 1953. He also produced and directed several swashbuckling adventure films for children, including *Treasure Island, Robin Hood, 20,000 Leagues Under the Sea* and *Davy Crockett.* Major features of these films were the high quality of production, artwork, scenery, music score – and a certain naïve zest. The films had a great appeal to children, though there was a tendency to fall back on sentimental stereotypes and folksy American values.

Mary Poppins released in 1964, was the most successful Disney film of the 1960s, and many hailed the live-action/animation combination feature as his greatest achievement.

> *"Of all our inventions for mass communication, pictures still speak the most universally understood language."*

A major feature of Walt Disney's career was his strong and voracious business sense. He was intent on making as much money as possible out of each project, and there were always tie-in books, toys and other merchandise that developed into a business that was as big as the films. The most spectacular tie-in projects were the Disney theme parks. Disneyland, one of the world's first theme parks opened in California in 1955.

However, Walt Disney tragically died of lung cancer in 1966, aged 65, during the planning stages for a second theme park – Disney World. But brother, Roy Disney, ensured that Walt's legacy lived on and continued the work, opening Walt Disney World's Magic Kingdom in 1971. Roy died shortly after, but the second phase of Walt Disney World went ahead and the Epcot theme park was opened in 1982. Today, what was known as the Florida Project is now the largest and most popular private-run tourist destination on the planet, where Walt Disney and Mickey Mouse are still remembered affectionately and loved by all the patrons. Walt once said, 'You can design and create, and build the most wonderful place in the world. But it takes people to make the dream a reality.'

Full of natural flair and talent, Walt Disney was a man of ideas and imagination. He liked to say he was in the business of making dreams come true, but he achieved what he did through ruthless determination, hard work and enormous self-confidence. He certainly made mistakes, and he experienced many severe setbacks, but he was irrepressible and he always tried again, and tried harder next time. Disney dominated the American movie industry in a unique way; he still holds the record for the largest number of Academy Award nominations (59) and the largest number of Oscars (22).

Responsible for transforming a minor art form, the black-and-white short cartoon film, into a virtuoso performance that escalated into a worldwide enterprise, Walt Disney was a one-man popular entertainment revolution.

> *"No matter how your heart is grieving, if you keep on believing, the dreams that you wish will come true."*

NATHANIEL DOMINY

The Changing Face of Human Evolution

QUOTE

"I never stop working. I'm always thinking."

BIOGRAPHY

NAME: Nathaniel J. Dominy

BORN: May 27, 1976

NATIONALITY: American

OCCUPATION: Anthropologist,
Evolutionary Biologist

Nathaniel Dominy is currently Professor of Anthropology at the University of California, Santa Cruz. He holds a BA in Anthropology and English Literature from Johns Hopkins University and a PhD in Anatomy from the University of Hong Kong. A gifted, dedicated teacher, Dominy is a committed researcher with some startling new ideas.

A young scientist, still in his thirties, Nathaniel Dominy seems set to shape the future. He has already made significant contributions to the study of human evolution. His investigations analyze the diet and nutrition of our early ancestors living around two million years ago. He believes around that time the human metabolism developed a unique nutritional advantage over the other primates.

Dominy stumbled on his research theme while he was on a college fact-finding trip to Costa Rica with his anatomy professors. He was a football player for Johns Hopkins University, and so he was assigned the physically demanding task of catching small monkeys as they fell, drugged, out of trees. 'You have this moving target, completely unconscious, and you have a net in your hand.' When he went back to Costa Rica the next summer, he found himself thinking about deciphering the monkeys' lifestyle and their eating habits – by studying their teeth. 'I got this quick introduction to the importance of food and diet in thinking about the adaptation and behaviours of primates and humans. I just loved every minute,' he said later.

Like a lot of scientists who make major breakthroughs, Nathaniel Dominy is working at the boundary of several disciplines; this is often the place where discoveries are made. He explores the crossroads where anthropology, ecology and genetics intersect – with a bit of archaeology thrown in. What he hopes to discover is what exactly led to, or fuelled, the development in human beings of large brains and bipedalism, the habit of walking on two feet rather than on all fours.

In 2009, Dominy was working on the question 'Why are some human populations taller than others?' He went to Uganda to collect DNA samples from two pygmy tribes, the Twa and the Sua. Once the whole of central Africa was clothed in rain forest. Dominy believes that these unusually short people would have found it easier to navigate inside the dense jungle environment, and also stay cooler. Dominy is surprised that no-one appears to have thought of it before. 'Body size is central to survival. It affects the kinds of things we eat, how we reproduce, our metabolism. Here we are in 2009, and we still don't know why it varies so much!' he said.

Research in central Africa has been part of a cross-continental investigation of pygmy populations to evaluate the costs of walking on two feet in terms of biomechanics and metabolism. In the early phase of the evolution of primitive humans, there was a slow and gradual increase in brain size. This change might be explained by gradually improving techniques of hunting, but then there was a surge in brain size about two million years ago, the moment when the genus Homo appeared.

Dominy says the change came when some pre-humans began eating certain foods. Modern human saliva contains abundant amylase, an enzyme that is good at digesting starch quickly. This means that modern human beings are able to digest starchy foods like seeds, bulbs, corms and tubers – plant material in the ground. So individuals with the ability to digest this otherwise quite indigestible food had a huge advantage, especially because tubers seem to grow everywhere.

His theory – and it is still only a theory – is that individuals or groups who inherited the 'amylase gene' were able to find food that they could eat wherever they journeyed. Migration became possible, because tubers could be found growing almost anywhere. Dominy believes that the long-held belief that meat was the staple food in the prehistoric diet is wrong. He points to the shape of human teeth as revealing that we are (still) better adapted to eating plant material than meat, and that our ancestors are likely to have been more dependent on tubers, fruit and honey than on meat.

In 1999, scientists analyzed the teeth of one of our primate ancestors, *Australopithecus africanus*, living three million years ago. The chemical make-up of the teeth showed that grass and grass-eating animals were important parts of the diet. But the size and shape of the teeth indicated something else – that our ancestors spent a lot of time munching hard and brittle root material like tubers.

In 2007, Dominy found more evidence – the teeth of both ancient and modern African mole rats that live almost entirely on bulbs have exactly the same chemical profiles to our own ancestors. This means that Dominy's theory has some evidence to support it. Eating tubers may have delivered enough energy to allow our ancestors to outwit carnivores, devise better ways to make tools, build shelters and to become inventors who changed the environment they lived in.

Nathaniel Dominy is in the middle of his career as a scientist, so it is too early even to evaluate his achievement. But, whether or not his exploration of ancient eating habits really does solve the mystery of human evolution, there can be no doubt that a brilliant mind is at work. However, the history of science is full of ideas and careers that have led nowhere or, frustratingly, have at the last moment been trumped by the work of other scientists. Only time will tell the impact that Nathaniel Dominy will have on the world.

"You learn more from a week in the forest than a semester in the classroom."

THOMAS EDISON

The Extraordinary Wizard of Invention

QUOTE

"Genius is one per cent inspiration, ninety-nine per cent perspiration."

BIOGRAPHY

NAME: Thomas Alva Edison

BORN: February 11, 1847
Milan, Ohio, United States

DIED: October 18, 1931 (Aged 84)
West Orange, New Jersey,
United States

NATIONALITY: American

OCCUPATION: Inventor, businessman

Thomas Alva Edison was born in Milan, Ohio, USA in 1847, the youngest of seven children. At school, Edison's mind wandered. His impatient teacher referred to him as 'addled', and young Tom's schooling came to an end after only three months. He might have gone through life seeing himself as a failure, but his mother had faith in him. 'My mother was the making of me,' he said, 'She was so true, so sure of me; and I felt I had something to live for, someone I must not disappoint.' His mother became his teacher. A great deal of his schooling came from reading Parker's *School of Natural Philosophy* and *The Cooper Union*.

Another setback was deafness, which may account for his apparent inattentiveness at school. The cause of the deafness is unclear. Legend has it that Edison was hit round the head by a conductor on a train, when his chemical laboratory in a boxcar caught fire, and he was thrown off the train along with his chemicals and apparatus. The story may be somewhat apocryphal, but it gained impetus as Edison's retelling became more embellished during his later years.

The Edison family moved to Port Huron in Michigan in 1854, when the railway bypassed Milan. Edison sold candy on trains running between Port Huron and Detroit, and managed to negotiate the exclusive rights to sell newspapers on the train. With four helpers, he printed his own *Grand Trunk Herald*, which he sold with his other papers. This was the first of Edison's ventures as an entrepreneur. He was eventually to found 14 companies. One of them, General Electric, still exists today and is among the biggest in the world.

After Edison saved a three-year-old boy from being killed by a train, the boy's father, J. U. Mackenzie, expressed his gratitude by training Edison as a telegraph operator. Soon he began inventing. His first patented invention was for an electric vote recorder in 1869. The first invention that drew public attention was his 1877 phonograph. This recorded on tinfoil wrapped round a grooved cylinder, but the sound quality was poor. A few years later Alexander Graham Bell and others produced an improved version using wax-coated cardboard cylinders. But in any case, Edison's major invention was probably the first industrial

research laboratory, built at Menlo Park, New Jersey (now rebuilt at the Henry Ford Museum in Dearborn).

The quadruplex telegraph was Edison's first major financial success and Menlo Park became a kind of an ideas factory for inventions, most of which were legally attributed to Edison, even though they were often the work of his staff. One of them was William Joseph Hammer, an electrical engineer who helped to develop several inventions, but worked mainly on the incandescent electric light. He was put in charge of testing and recording the results. In 1880, Edison made him chief engineer at the Edison Lamp Works which, in the first year, produced 50,000 light bulbs. Edison admitted that Hammer was 'a pioneer of incandescent lighting', but did not go so far as to call him 'the pioneer'.

> *"To invent, you need a good imagination and a pile of junk."*

Most of Edison's patents were for inventions that improved 'prior art'. The light bulb was a case in point; incandescent lamps had already been invented, by a number of scientists including the English inventors Humphry Davy and Joseph Swan, but Edison produced a variation that was usable, practical and cheap. The phonograph patent was unprecedented, in describing Edison's machine as the first device to record and reproduce sounds. As far as the light bulb was concerned, Swan's existing patent was a problem to Edison's commercial exploitation of the idea. Edison

Thomas Edison in his
Menlo Park laboratory.

was forced to negotiate a partnership with Swan (Ediswan).

The mass production of light bulbs that followed was a major part of the necessary infrastructure for electric power. In 1880, Edison patented a system for electricity distribution, another piece of the infrastructure. In 1882, he launched his Pearl Street generating station; it served just 59 customers in Manhattan, but it was a beginning. By 1887 there were 121 Edison power stations in America. Edison said, 'We will make electricity so cheap that only the rich will use candles.'

The Menlo Park laboratory expanded to cover two city blocks, stocked with almost every conceivable material an inventor could want. Edison placed a quotation from Joshua Reynolds over his desk and at several points round the facility: 'There is no expedient to which a man will not resort to avoid the real labor of thinking.'

The idea was to use thought to create knowledge, and then control its application. Edison was brilliant at lateral thinking when trawling for ideas, and equally brilliant at applying them. It was idly examining a few threads from a bamboo fishing rod that gave him the idea of using a carbonized bamboo filament for his light bulb; he found that such a filament could last over 1,200 hours.

Edison invented the carbon microphone, which was used in all telephones along with the Bell receiver – until the 1980s. Here again Edison had a fight for primacy; in the end a court ruled that Edison was the inventor, not Emile Berliner. Crucial to Edison's success was his ability to pair mass-production with intellectual property rights.

Edison designed the first commercially available fluoroscope, a machine that uses X-rays to take radiographs. This system produced brighter images than those Röntgen was able to produce. Edison was aware of the dangers of equipment like this; 'Don't talk to me about X-rays. I am afraid of them,' he said after one of his workers had died due to excessive exposure to them.

"I have not failed. I've just found 10,000 ways that won't work."

Another of his employees was Nikola Tesla, who was assigned the task of improving the electricity generators. When Tesla had done this and asked for the $50,000 he claimed Edison had promised him, Edison cruelly replied, 'When you become a full-fledged American, you will appreciate an American joke.' Tesla resigned and held a grudge against Edison all his life. When Edison died, Tesla was contemptuous; 'He had no hobby, cared for no sort of amusement and lived in utter disregard of the most elementary rules of hygiene ... His method was inefficient in the extreme; a little theory and calculation would have saved him 90% of the labour. But he had a contempt for book learning and mathematical knowledge, trusting entirely to his inventor's instinct.'

When Edison was close to death, he said, looking back, that the biggest mistake he had made was in not respecting Tesla or his work. In 1915, *The New York Times* announced that Edison and Tesla were to receive a Nobel Prize jointly. But it did not happen. Perhaps the prize committee realized there was a risk of embarrassment: they awarded the prize instead to W. H. Bragg and W. L. Bragg for their X-ray analysis of crystal structure.

The darker side of Edison is illustrated by another episode from 1902. Edison's agents in London pirated the pioneering film *A Trip to the Moon* by George Méliès. Edison made hundreds of copies and showed them in New York. Poor Méliès received nothing in compensation and went bankrupt. Edison also enjoyed the highly controversial 1915 American silent drama, *The Birth of a Nation*, portraying the founding of the Ku Klux Klan in the southern states of America, and showing the Klan as heroic force for good versus the evil of African-Americans. The movie was banned in several US cities due to its racism. Perhaps partly because of his deafness, Edison went on preferring silent films – talkies 'spoilt everything,' he said.

In the 1920s, Edison and Henry Ford, the car manufacturer, became close friends. Edison's countless devices greatly influenced the world. Many were small and trivial, like the kinetoscope (a What the Butler Saw arcade peepshow) while some changed life for millions, like the electric light bulb. In old age, Edison revisited his birthplace in Milan, Ohio; he was shocked to find that it was still lit with lamps and candles – yet he himself had owned it since 1906!

"Our greatest weakness lies in giving up. The most certain way to succeed is always to try just one more time."

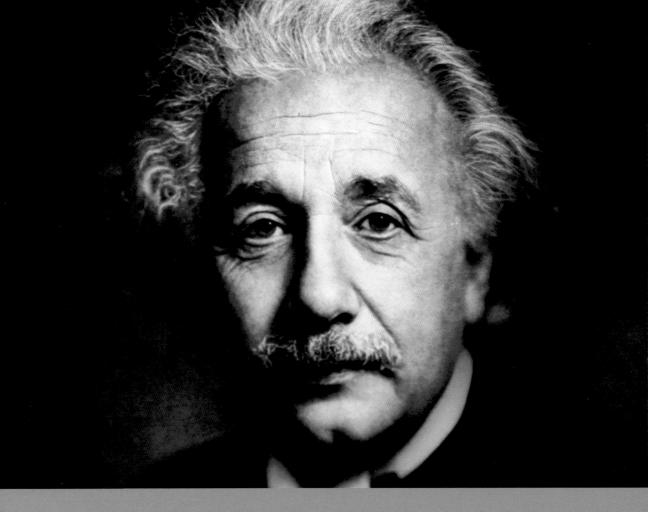

ALBERT EINSTEIN

The Defining Genius of the 20th Century

QUOTE ━━━

*"Only two things are infinite: the universe and human
stupidity – and I'm not sure about the universe."*

BIOGRAPHY ━━━

NAME: Albert Einstein

BORN: March 14, 1879
Ulm, Württemberg,
German Empire

DIED: April 18, 1955 (Aged 76)
Princeton, New Jersey,
United States

NATIONALITY: Swiss-American

OCCUPATION: Theoretical physicist

Albert Einstein was born in Ulm, Germany in 1879, the son of a German-Jewish industrialist. He attended school at Aarau in Switzerland and then the Polytechnic School in Zürich, going on to study mathematics at Zürich University. After graduation he earned a PhD. Einstein considered taking up geography, but decided the subject was too difficult; it is interesting to speculate what might have happened, in both geography and physics, if Einstein had followed this alternative path. We can never know what would have happened if people had followed different career paths, and this is one of many problems that we face in measuring the impact of individuals on the world.

During the time when he was studying for his doctorate, Einstein worked in the Swiss patent office. It was while he was working in the patent office in 1905 that Einstein published his first, restricted, theory of relativity.

He formulated the theory in response to the difficulties encountered by Michelson and Morley when they tried to measure the absolute value of the Earth's movement through space. They came up with a negative result, and put this down to a property of light. This prompted Einstein to put forward the idea that, if the speed of light were taken as a constant, the same as measured by all observers, anywhere and moving in any direction, that would require a modification of Newtonian mechanics. Until that moment, Newton's model was the standard model in physics. Einstein also proved mathematically that nothing could move faster than the speed of light, that objects must become shorter and shorter as they approach that speed, and that clocks would slow down and stop as they approached the speed of light.

Some of these propositions had been put forward before, but as absurdities, as if to say, about another proposition, 'So that can't be true.' Einstein was putting them forward as actual properties of the universe. At the time, there were no means of testing his theory, and only a few German mathematicians accepted what he was saying.

Ten years afterwards, Einstein put forward his epoch-making general theory of relativity. In this, Einstein added the idea that gravitation might affect measurements through space and time. He also suggested that observations already made might be used to demonstrate this, such as the observed irregularity in the orbit of Mercury, and the slight shift in positions of stars when they were observed close to the sun. The differences in position were very slight, but enough to suggest that gravitation might bend light. Measurements of high-speed electrons were showing changes in mass that agreed with Einstein's formulae.

Because of real-world evidence Einstein was able to offer, his theory was given much more serious attention from scientists everywhere. One important implication was that the two forms of universal energy readily available for measurement, mass and the energy locked up in matter, were in a sense equivalent. The energy locked up in matter, E, was equal to its mass, m, multiplied by the square of the velocity of radiation, c. This simple formula, $E = mc^2$, has become the most famous equation of all time.

Pierre and Marie Curie had already realized that vast amounts of energy were locked up in matter, but it did not occur to them that that energy was accessible, that it might be released. It certainly occurred to Einstein, and the functioning of his brilliant mind was key in a long intellectual chain reaction that led to the releasing and harnessing of nuclear energy. It remained for Rutherford to verify Einstein's formula experimentally; for James Chadwick to discover the neutron; for Enrico Fermi to transmute half the elements in the atomic table; for Otto Hahn and others to recognize that a certain uranium isotope might be split; and for Fermi to design the first nuclear reactor. But Einstein took the first step, which was as much a leap of the imagination as it was a result of calculation.

From 1916 (when he was 37) onwards, Einstein spent much of his own energy on trying to find a 'Theory of Everything'. He searched for an all-inclusive explanation of the energy in all phenomena in one all-embracing unified theory. Was this a brilliant mind over-stretching itself, over-reaching? He finally published his theory in 1953, but it did not meet with general acceptance. Einstein himself expressed dissatisfaction with it in that he had been unable to come up with any way of testing it experimentally.

> *"The true sign of intelligence is not knowledge but imagination."*

Einstein was not just the creator or discoverer of relativity. He extended Max Planck's quantum theory and made major contributions in other areas of mathematics and physics. His discovery of the law of photoelectric effect became one of the bases of modern electronics, and for this – not for relativity – he was awarded the Nobel Prize for Physics in 1921.

Einstein became a Swiss citizen as a young man, but in 1913 he returned to Germany to become director of the Kaiser Wilhelm Physical Institute. In 1932, he was offered a post at the Institute for Advanced Study at Princeton, New Jersey. He accepted this job offer straight away but, when it became clear to him later that year that the anti-Semitic Hitler was about to come to power, he set sail for America without further delay. He became an American citizen in 1940, by which stage there was no foreseeable possibility for a scientist of Jewish family returning to Europe.

In August 1939, Einstein and Leó Szilárd wrote a letter to President Franklin D. Roosevelt outlining the possibility of constructing a new and powerful weapon.

Roosevelt was very interested and promptly set up the Manhattan Project to investigate the possibilities of developing the atomic bomb. There was an irony here, in that Einstein was a confirmed pacifist; on this basis, though a German by birth, he had opposed Germany's invasion of Belgium at the beginning of World War I.

> *"The world is a dangerous place to live; not because of the people who are evil, but because of the people who don't do anything about it."*

He was a great exponent of Zionism, socialism, world government and total disarmament, yet he knowingly set in motion the research project that culminated in the nuclear bombs that annihilated Hiroshima and Nagasaki, and the huge arsenals of nuclear missiles that gave the Cold War its icy bite. But Einstein's recommendation was made in the knowledge that the Nazis were probably planning to build an atomic bomb. The letter was in reality intended as a warning to Roosevelt – unless America developed the atomic bomb, the Germans would gain a huge military advantage.

Geniuses are as full of character flaws as the rest of us; indeed it is a reassuring source of relief when we discover they are just another human being. Einstein was certainly a genius, and perhaps *the* defining genius of the 20th century, yet he embodied these fundamental self-contradictions. Perhaps we should see them not as flaws, but as personal eccentricities – they are what make us all individuals. What Einstein did that was so extraordinary was to replace Newton's mechanical model and propose nothing less than a revolutionary new model for the universe and the way it works. A century on from when it was proposed, it has more than withstood the test of time.

> *"Logic will get you from A to B - Imagination will take you everywhere."*

ENRICO FERMI

A Beautiful Mind and the Terrible Bomb

QUOTE ▬▬▬▬▬▬▬▬▬▬▬▬▬▬▬▬▬▬▬▬▬▬▬▬▬▬▬▬▬▬▬▬▬▬

"There are two possible outcomes: if the result confirms the hypothesis, then you've made a measurement. If the result is contrary to the hypothesis, then you've made a discovery."

BIOGRAPHY ▬▬▬▬▬▬▬▬▬▬▬▬▬▬▬▬▬▬▬▬▬▬▬▬▬▬▬▬▬▬▬▬▬

NAME: Enrico Fermi

BORN: September 29, 1901
Rome, Italy

DIED: November 28, 1954 (Aged 53)
Chicago, Illinois, United States

NATIONALITY: Italian / American

OCCUPATION: Theoretical / experimental physicist, Father of the Atomic Bomb

Enrico Fermi was born in Rome in 1901, where his father worked for the Ministry of Communications. His mother was a junior school teacher, who built her own pressure cooker. Enrico and his brother Giulio seem to have inherited their mother's mechanical ingenuity; they dismantled small engines to see how they worked. When Giulio died suddenly in 1915, Enrico was deeply upset and immersed himself in his scientific studies as a distraction from grief.

Fermi's first encounter with physics was through a book he found at the local market. It was a 900-page book, written in Latin, *Elementorum physicae mathematicae*, and it covered a wide spectrum of scientific subjects: mathematics, astronomy, optics and acoustics. The marginal notes Fermi wrote in it show that he studied it intensely. Then Fermi made friends with another boy who was interested in science, Enrico Persico, and together they built gyroscopes and measured the Earth's magnetic field. The young Fermi was further encouraged by a friend of his father, Adolfo Amidei, who gave him several books on physics, which he quickly assimilated.

In 1918, Fermi went to the *Scuola Normale Superiore* in Pisa. This was where he would gain both his degree and his doctorate. Candidates had to sit an entrance exam which included an essay. On the subject *Characteristics of Sound*, Fermi decided to derive and solve a complex equation relating to waves on a string. The examiner was impressed; the 17-year-old had produced a piece of work of doctoral standard. Fermi was already showing prodigious ability. Fermi found new friends at the college, including Franco Rasetti, who later became a close friend and scientific collaborator.

From 1919 to 1923, Fermi became familiar with the latest ideas on general relativity, quantum mechanics and atomic physics. His knowledge of quantum physics became so advanced that the head of the Physics Institute, Professor Puccianti, asked him to run seminars on the subject. When he was in his third year at university, in 1921, Fermi began publishing his revolutionary new ideas in two scientific papers in the Italian journal *Nuovo Cimento*. He was able, shortly afterwards to offer evidence that his ideas were valid, and a new paper was published; this was well received, and translated into German then republished in the prestigious *Physikalische Zeitschrift*.

In 1922 he published his paper *On Phenomena that Happen Close to the Line of Time*, in which he introduced the so-called Fermi Coordinates. And this was happening just at the time when Fermi graduated! He was already stretching the limits of his subject. The following year, he wrote an appendix for *The Mathematical Theory of Relativity* by Kopff, and in it he pointed out, for the first time, that within Einstein's famous equation $E = mc^2$ there was an enormous amount of nuclear potential energy available for exploitation. Here, in 1923, were the seeds of the idea of nuclear energy. As a postgraduate student, Fermi worked at Göttingen, Leiden and Florence before becoming Professor of Atomic Physics at the University of Rome. Fermi, the virtuoso student, was still only 24 years old. Professor Corbino helped Fermi assemble a team of scientists who became known as 'The Via Panisperna Boys'. This group made significant advances in both theoretical and experimental physics. In their experiments bombarding elements with neutrons, they narrowly missed observing nuclear fission in uranium; at that time, on the basis of calculations, Fermi thought fission in a heavier atom improbable if not impossible.

Fermi proceeded methodically, using mathematical reasoning to produce a complete solution to the problem he was exploring, then setting up the experiment to demonstrate the solution. From boyhood on, Fermi carefully recorded his calculations in notebooks, returning to them later to

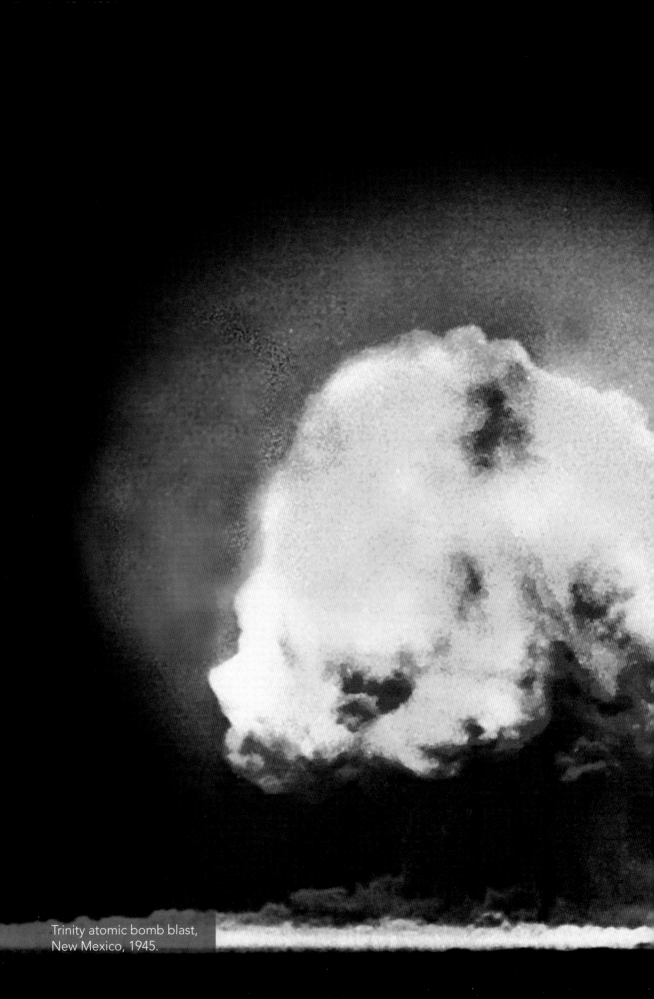

Trinity atomic bomb blast,
New Mexico, 1945.

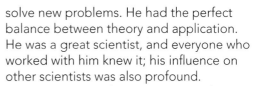

solve new problems. He had the perfect balance between theory and application. He was a great scientist, and everyone who worked with him knew it; his influence on other scientists was also profound.

He went on working in Rome until 1938. In that year he went to Stockholm to receive the Nobel Prize in Physics and then emigrated, with his wife and children, to New York. His main reason for emigrating was Mussolini's Manifesto of Race; the new laws were a threat to Fermi's Jewish wife Laura, and they put most of Fermi's assistants out of work.

"It is no good to try to stop knowledge from going forward."

In America, Fermi quickly found work at Columbia University. In December 1938, Hahn and Strassmann, two German scientists reported that they had apparently produced nuclear fission in their experiments. The experiment was repeated and the results were carried to the US by Niels Bohr, when he went to lecture at Princeton. From there, the news travelled to Fermi, and it was not long before Bohr went to Columbia to see Fermi. From this meeting it became clear that the Columbia University team should try using neutron bombardment to measure the energy released in the nuclear fission of uranium.

Fermi and five other scientists carried out the first nuclear fission experiment in America in January 1939. Then Fermi went to the University of Chicago where, with President Franklin D. Roosevelt's go-ahead, the first nuclear reactor was constructed, in a display of Fermi's meticulous calculation and planning. Known as Chicago Pile-1, it was Fermi's work that made possible this landmark in the development of nuclear energy. In December 1942 Fermi finally succeeded in producing and controlling a fission chain reaction in this reactor pile at Chicago.

The report of the successful chain reaction to the National Defense Research

Committee was coded. The message ran, 'The Italian navigator has landed in the New World.' Fermi had become the new Columbus. Not long after this, the reactor project was dovetailed into the US Government research that developed the first atomic bomb during World War II. In 1943, Fermi was asked to join the secret laboratory team working on the bomb directed by Robert Oppenheimer at Los Alamos, New Mexico.

The first atomic bomb was detonated at 5.30 am on July 16, 1945, at the Alamogordo air base 120 miles (193 km) south of Albuquerque, New Mexico. It was discharged on top of a steel tower surrounded by scientific equipment. The tower was completely vaporized and the surrounding desert surface fused to glass for a radius of 800 yards (730 m). The following month, two more of the project's atomic bombs were dropped on Hiroshima and Nagasaki, Japan, to end World War II.

Fermi's genius is hard to exaggerate. C. P. Snow said, 'If Fermi had been born a few years earlier, one could well imagine him discovering Rutherford's atomic nucleus and then developing Bohr's theory of the hydrogen atom. If this sounds like hyperbole, anything about Fermi is likely to sound like hyperbole.' Fermi's brilliance was paralleled by his practicality: he always assessed what was possible. He did not like complicated theories.

Although he had great abilities as a mathematician, he would avoid elaborate calculations if there was a simpler way forward. His preference for back-of-the-envelope calculations became known as 'The Fermi Method'. Perhaps the classic example of this was when Fermi observed the Trinity test of the atomic bomb in July 1945; he released confetti into the shock wave to estimate the yield of that first nuclear explosion.

He was also, unusually modest for a high achiever. It seems that everyone who worked with him liked him, from technicians to Nobel Prize winners. On one occasion Fermi was even seen helping a Princeton student move a table, obediently taking instructions where to place it.

However his beautiful mind was well suited to higher plane doodling as well and he mused constantly on what is now known as *Fermi's Paradox* –

"There are billions of star systems in the universe. We would expect that intelligent life in at least one of them would have made contact with us by now ..."

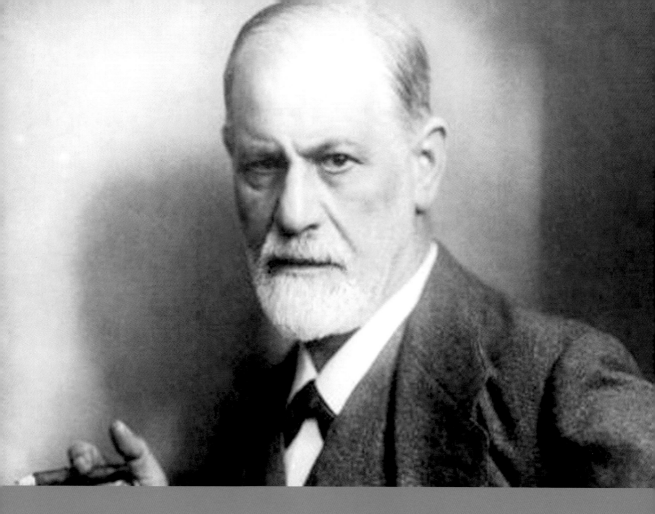

SIGMUND FREUD

Betraying Our Innermost Secrets

BIOGRAPHY ━━━━━━━━━━━━━━━━━━━━━━━━━━━━━━━━━

NAME: Sigismund Schlomo Freud

BORN: May 6, 1856
Freiberg in Mähren, Moravia,
Austrian Empire (now Příbor,
Czech Republic)

DIED: September 23, 1939 (Aged 83)
London, England,
United Kingdom

NATIONALITY: Austrian

OCCUPATION: Neurologist

Sigmund Freud was born at Freiberg in Mähren in Moravia, which in the 19th century was part of the Austrian Empire. His father Jacob was a poor Jewish wool merchant. His mother Amalie was Jacob's third wife and 20 years his junior. In spite of their poverty, they made sure that Sigmund was educated. Motivated by reading Goethe, Freud decided to study medicine in Vienna. Money became a problem and he had to put his research to one side and began work as a clinical neurologist.

In 1884, an Austrian neurologist called Josef Breuer told Freud of an experience in which hysteria was cured by using hypnosis to help a patient recall painful past experiences. It was a turning-point for Freud. He was profoundly impressed by Breuer's cathartic technique and developed it until it became the foundation stone of modern psychoanalysis.

Then, in 1885, Freud moved to Paris to study under Jean-Martin Charcot. He switched from treating hysteria as a neurological problem to treating it from a psychological point of view. Freud was changing from neurologist to psychoanalyst.

Returning to Vienna, he developed a new psychiatric technique – free association. He started using this instead of hypnosis to find out what was beneath the surface of the patient's mind, and so gradually refined psychoanalysis as a method of treatment.

In 1893, he persuaded Breuer that he ought to publish his breakthrough in the treatment of hysteria, and in 1895, Freud and Breuer in collaboration published a book called *Studies in Hysteria*. In 1897, their collaboration ended in disagreement over Freud's theory of infantile sexuality. Freud tried the patience of many of his friends and colleagues as he developed his revolutionary and often shocking ideas. Many of them thought he was too insistent on the role of sex in the mind, and especially on the role of repressed sexual urges. This obsession was very plain to see in his published work.

In 1900, he published his landmark work, *The Interpretation of Dreams*, in which he argued that dreams are disguised manifestations of repressed sexual desires.

His ideas excited enormous interest, and a great deal of controversy.

In 1902, he was appointed Extraordinary Professor of Neuropathology at Vienna University. He also began holding weekly seminars at his home, for all those adventurously exploring the human psyche including Alfred Adler, Ernest Jones and Carl Gustav Jung.

In 1905, the publication of his *Three Essays on Sexuality* met with intense and uncomprehending opposition. The pattern seemed to be set.

In 1908, the informal weekly meetings at his home became formalized into the Vienna Psychoanalytical Society, which changed its name in 1910 to the International Psychoanalytical Association. Freud's most distinguished protégé, Jung, was its first president who in 1908 chaired the first International Congress of Psychoanalysis. Through publications and conferences, Freud's ideas were spreading round the world.

> *"The great question that has never been answered, and which I have not yet been able to answer, despite my thirty years of research ... is 'What does a woman want?'"*

Freud's views were extremely doctrinaire and dogmatic and it was almost inevitable that several of his pupils would disagree with him so strongly that they would part company. Adler left in 1910. Jung broke with Freud in 1913. The problem was that, having found his explanation for neuroses, Freud was not prepared to keep an open mind.

He felt threatened by Jung and on two occasions, when he thought Jung's remarks revealed a death-wish against him, Freud fainted on the spot.

Even so, Freud was not put off by the departure of disciples or the loss of friends. He produced *Totem and Taboo* in 1913, *Beyond the Pleasure Principle* in 1920 and *Ego and Id* in 1923. Freud saw the human unconscious mind as divided into three compartments, the *id*, the *ego* and the *super-ego*. In 1927, he published a controversial view of religion, *The Future of an Illusion*.

With the rise of the Nazis and the Third Reich during the 1930s, Freud became more preoccupied with the European situation. Together with Einstein, Freud wrote *Why War?* in 1933. Psychoanalysis was outlawed under Nazi rule, so it was difficult professionally for him to continue. Despite advancing age and infirmity, Freud continued to be as active as he could be, directing the *International Journal of Psychology*.

When Austria was invaded by Hitler in 1938, arrangements were made to rescue Freud, a prominent and conspicuously Jewish intellectual who was clearly in mortal danger from the Nazis. The Freud family escaped to a new home in Hampstead, north London where he produced one more major work. *Moses and Monotheism* explored the psychology of anti-Semitism. But he died of cancer not long after his arrival in England, in September 1939.

Freud's single most important discovery was the existence of the unconscious mind and its powerful and dynamic influence on the conscious mind. Closely connected with this idea is the concept of the mind being split into layers due to inner conflict among the various psychic forces within the mind.

One of the psychic forces, 'repression', is behind the well-known term 'Freudian Slip' which has found its way into everyday speech. Named by Freud as parapraxis, it is an unintentional slip of the tongue that listeners interpret as the expression of a repressed wish, usually causing embarrassment to the verbalizer. Freud, himself, referred to these slips as *Fehlleistungen* meaning 'misperformance'.

> *"These phenomena are not accidental … they have a meaning and can be interpreted, one is justified in inferring from them the presence of restrained or repressed impulses and intentions."*

Another Freudian idea was the existence of infantile sexuality, still a controversial idea, and the complex jealousies that children feel towards their parents which he called 'The Oedipus Complex'.

Freud's influence spread beyond the specialist practitioners of psychoanalysis. Medics, philosophers, artists, novelists and playwrights worldwide recognized that a whole new way of thinking about the human mind – and therefore thinking about the human race – had come into being. Freudian psychology, for better or worse, came to dominate many aspects of the 20th century shaping all our views of human habits and ways of behaving – conscious or unconscious.

"Words have a magical power. They can bring either the greatest happiness or deepest despair."

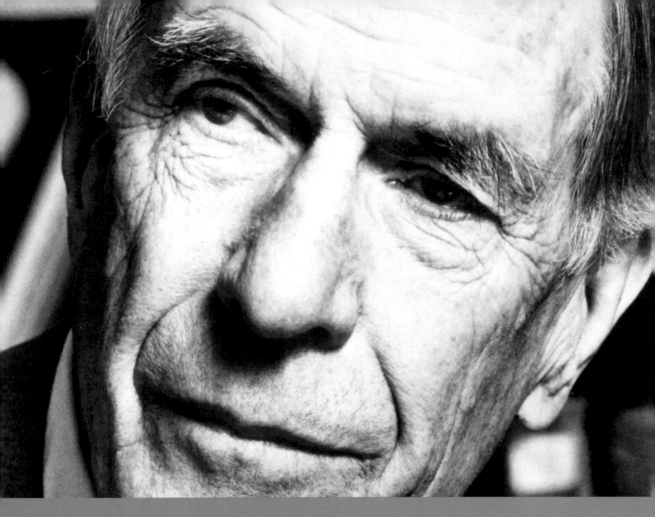

JOHN KENNETH GALBRAITH

The Birth of Conventional Wisdom

QUOTE

"Politics is the art of choosing between the disastrous and the unpalatable."

BIOGRAPHY

NAME: John Kenneth Galbraith

BORN: October 15, 1908
Iona Station, Ontario, Canada

DIED: April 29, 2006 (Aged 97)
Cambridge, Massachusetts,
United States

NATIONALITY: American

OCCUPATION: Economist, public official,
diplomat

John Kenneth Galbraith was born into a Scottish-Canadian family and brought up on the family farm in Dunwich Township, Ontario. His father was a farmer and schoolteacher, his mother a political activist. Galbraith's first great achievement was growing to the astonishing height of 6ft 8in (2.3 m). Then he graduated from Ontario Agricultural College with a BSc in agricultural economics. In 1933, he earned an MSc and in 1934 a PhD in Agricultural economics at the University of California, Berkeley. In 1937 he acquired US citizenship, giving up his British citizenship, and at the same time spent a year in England at the University of Cambridge, where he came under the influence of John Maynard Keynes. Galbraith taught at Harvard and Princeton and in 1949 became Professor of Economics at Harvard.

In World War II, Galbraith was deputy head of the Office of Price Administration; his task was to maintain price stability, and prevent inflation from crippling the war effort. In this he was successful, but opposition from conservatives in Congress and from business interests acted against him and he was forced out in 1943, accused of 'communistic tendencies'. Galbraith was immediately taken on by *Fortune* magazine, where he was able to expound Keynesian economics to the leaders of American business. For a time in 1946 he worked in the State Department as director of the Office of Economic Security Policy. He was supposed to be in charge of economic affairs relating to Germany, Japan, Austria and South Korea, but he was not trusted by senior diplomats, who saw him as too left wing. Galbraith was in favour of having a more relaxed relationship with the Soviet Union, but this was not in line with the government's current containment policy. Galbraith gave up and went back to journalism. In 1947, with Hubert Humphrey and Eleanor Roosevelt, he co-founded Americans for Democratic Action.

Galbraith became an adviser to President John F. Kennedy and US Ambassador to India from 1961 to 1963. He had a close rapport with Kennedy and was able to send his cables direct to the President. He developed a similar rapport with Nehru, the Indian Prime Minister, and advised him on economic matters. He was a harsh critic of Lord Mountbatten's passivity at the time of the Partition of India in 1947 and the bloodshed that went with it. Long after leaving office, Galbraith went on supporting India; every year on graduation day at Harvard he gave a lunch for Indian students.

"Economics is not an exact science."

In 1972, Galbraith became president of the American Economic Association. In 2000 he was awarded the US Presidential Medal of Freedom and the Leontief Prize for his outstanding contribution to economic theory. In 2001, he was awarded the Padma Vibhushan, the second highest award in India, for his work in strengthening ties between India and the US. These late honours were added to his 50 honorary degrees from all round the world.

Some economists regarded Galbraith as an iconoclast. He rejected the mathematical models of neoclassical economics as divorced from reality. He believed that economic activity could not be boiled down into inviolable laws. Instead he saw it as a complex process, a product of the culture and politics of the time. He believed that significant areas – advertising, the separation between corporate ownership and management, the influence of government and military spending – were persistently overlooked by many economists, largely because they were not reducible to axioms or laws.

He was a brilliantly clear writer, who wrote several best-selling books and hundreds of essays. He was a great publicist for economics, contributing to a major PBS and BBC television series in 1977, *The Age of Uncertainty*. He also had a vision of how the American economy would function in the future, as a three-sided structure – big business, big labour (lobby groups and unions) and an activist government. These three forces were benign and necessary to keep an economy in balance. This was very different from the economy of the pre-Depression era, where big business had almost total control. But this three-way counterbalancing did not happen in his lifetime. In a TV interview given shortly before he died, he commented, 'There's no question that this is a time when corporations have taken over the basic process of governing.'

Perhaps his most famous work was *The Affluent Society* (1958), in which he advocated that America should make large investments in highways and education, using capital raised from taxes. He coined the phrase 'conventional wisdom' when challenging the idea that continually increasing material production is a sign of a healthy economy and society. He was therefore one of the first post-materialists.

Many economists admired and respected Galbraith, but some hated what he was saying, among them Milton Friedman. He wrote, 'Many reformers – Galbraith is not alone in this – have as their basic objection to a free market that it frustrates them in achieving their reforms, because it enables people to have what they want, not what the reformers want. Hence every reformer has a strong tendency to be averse to a free market.'

Galbraith was a debunker, a demystifier. In 1975 he wrote, 'The study of money, above all other fields in economics, is one in which complexity is used to disguise truth or to evade truth, not to reveal it. The process by which banks create money is so simple the mind is repelled. With something so important, a deeper mystery seems only decent.'

Galbraith lived for nearly a hundred years and witnessed almost all of the 20th century. He died aged 97, a great writer and expounder of bracing ideas, he was still capable, sometimes in the midst of a very serious proposition, of making a sharply-observed witticism.

> **"Under capitalism, man exploits man. Under communism, it's just the opposite."**

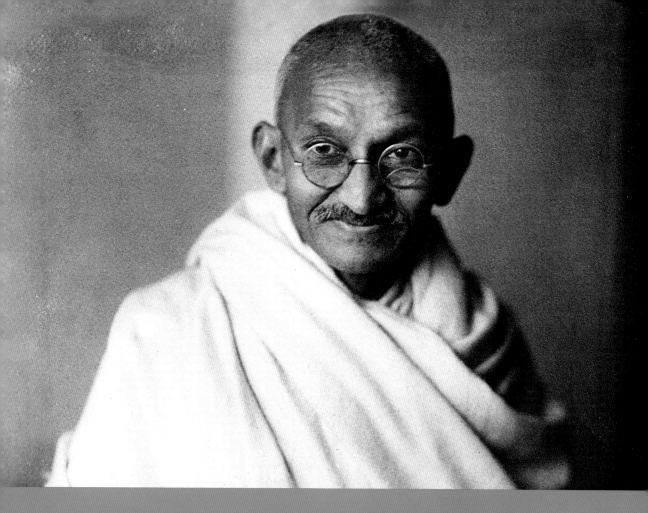

MOHANDAS GANDHI

Empowering the Deepest Convictions

QUOTE

"Live as if you were to die tomorrow – Learn as if you were to live forever."

BIOGRAPHY

NAME: Mohandas Karamchand Gandhi

BORN: October 2, 1869
Porbandar, Kathiawar Agency,
British India Empire

DIED: January 30, 1948 (Aged 78)
New Delhi, India

NATIONALITY: Indian

OCCUPATION: Indian nationalist, theorist
and organizer

Mohandas Gandhi was born into a Hindu family at Porbandar in western India. His father was chief minister of one of the Gujarat states. When he was 18, Mohandas was sent by his family to study law in London, where he was called to the bar in 1891. By this stage, the young man was already showing signs of the asceticism and extremism that would come to the fore and dominate his later life. On the voyage to England he almost starved, having promised his mother he would not eat meat. Once in London, he became an active member of the Vegetarian Society. This marked the beginning of a lifelong concern with diet, personal hygiene and moral scruple.

Once he had qualified as a lawyer, Gandhi set up a legal practice in Bombay, but he lacked the necessary confidence to be successful. In 1893, he gave up the practice, which was yielding an income of £5,000 a year, in order to live on one pound a week in South Africa. There he neglected his legal practice and devoted 21 years to opposing laws that discriminated against Indians. Gandhi and his friends set up a self-supporting commune, which they named Tolstoy Farm; the idea was to free themselves from dependence on the rest of the community. As his ideas about social reform developed, Gandhi was profoundly influenced by the writings of Leo Tolstoy, with whom he corresponded, and John Ruskin. The deepest influences on him were the *New Testament* and the *Bhagavad Gita*.

While he was struggling against the authorities in South Africa, Gandhi was arrested, imprisoned and beaten. At this time he was still a supporter of the British Empire, seeing the British influence as mainly benign.

The South African struggle reached a climax when, in 1913, a series of repressive measures culminated in a demand that every Indian seeking to live in the Transvaal must register. Gandhi organized a typical protest event, in which 2,000 Indians rallied behind him, and he led them repeatedly backwards and forwards across the Transvaal border. It was what would later be termed a publicity stunt – but it was effective. Public opinion swung behind the well-behaved Indians, and the oppressive measures were repealed. Gandhi also gained the respect of General Jan Smuts, who had initially done his best to crush the movement.

By 1914, Gandhi felt that the Indians in South Africa no longer needed his support and he returned to India. He supported Britain through World War I, but was at the same time taking increasing interest in the Congress movement for home rule for India. He soon came to dominate the movement. His civil disobedience campaign of 1920 created serious and violent disorder, and in 1922 he was imprisoned for two years for conspiracy. While he was in prison, relations between the Hindu and Muslim communities deteriorated conspicuously.

"Be the change that you wish to see in the world."

Gandhi disagreed with the Congress leaders' acceptance of proposals that they should join the new legislatures. In protest, he announced that he was retiring from politics for a year; in fact he dropped out for several years. During this time he toured villages, teaching people the principle of self-help, urging them to take up spinning as a way of escaping absolute poverty. He also urged them to abandon the caste system.

At each village meeting he addressed, he found that the organizers had divided audiences into two, caste people and untouchables. To counteract this, he always went and sat with the untouchables to speak. He also fought against alcohol and drug-taking, urging people to take proper care of their cattle and to develop goodwill between the religious communities. All of this added up to what he called 'the constructive programme', a crusade that was a preparation of India for the freedom struggle to come.

In 1930, Gandhi led a 240-mile march from his ashram (settlement) near Ahmedabad to the coast at Dandi, to make salt from the sea. The salt march was a symbolic gesture defying the government monopoly on salt, and it had an electrifying effect on the whole country. This led to his arrest. On release from prison in 1931, Gandhi relaunched his civil disobedience campaign in protest against the compromise measures that were being introduced. Another political weapon he used at this time was fasting. He threatened to 'fast unto death' when one of the new measures in effect condoned the different treatment of untouchables.

> *"You can chain me, you can torture me, you can even destroy this body, but you will never imprison my mind."*

When World War II broke out, Gandhi wanted to support the British against Nazi Germany, but gave in to Congress pressure, insisting that India would only cooperate if it was promised full independence. No promise was forthcoming from Britain. He began pressing more and more vehemently for complete independence. By 1942, Stafford Cripps, for the British government, assured India of independence on certain conditions once the war was over, but Gandhi dismissed this promise as 'a post-dated cheque'.

In 1944, Gandhi tried to establish an understanding with Jinnah, the Muslim leader, who was demanding an independent Muslim state. Gandhi and Jinnah could not agree. Gandhi's ideal was one, undivided India – but it was an unachievable ideal. By early 1947, a Partition of India was agreed by the Congress leaders, in spite of Gandhi's disapproval. By May 1947, Gandhi was ready to praise Britain's decision to give India independence as 'the noblest act of the British nation'. But independence was sullied by outbreaks of violence between Hindu and Muslim communities.

The strife between the communities could only be resolved by separating them, and creating a separate Muslim state of Pakistan (East and West) on either side of a predominantly Hindu India. Gandhi's promotion of home rule for India resulted not just in independence for the sub-continent, but the disintegration of the British Empire. India was, inevitably, just the first of the British possessions to wrest itself free.

In the midst of all this, Gandhi himself became the victim of an almost random act of violence. In January 1948 he was shot dead by a Hindu extremist who believed that as long as Gandhi lived India would never be Hindu-dominated.

Gandhi, the 'great soul', was venerated by many as a great moral teacher who wanted to free India from the British, but also from materialism and from caste prejudice. In many ways, his mission was nearer to that of Jesus than anything else in modern times. He tried certain techniques, such as non-violent resistance, and found they worked, so he repeated them. Was this brilliance of mind, or brilliance of spirit?

His critics saw him as deluded, blind to the violence to which his 'non-violent' campaigns would lead. Overall, he is seen as a great force for peace, progress and justice, with a message not just for India but for the rest of the world. His grass roots, self-help approach to social and economic development with hindsight looks very progressive and far-sighted. He was, perhaps unintentionally, looking into the future, finding a way forward for the 21st century.

> *"The weak can never forgive. Forgiveness is the attribute of the strong."*

Mohandas Gandhi leading the salt march in India for freedom from British rule, 1930.

BILL GATES

Business @ the Speed of Thought

"Your most unhappy customers are your greatest source of learning."

NAME: William Henry Gates III

BORN: October 28, 1955
Seattle, Washington,
United States

NATIONALITY: American

OCCUPATION: Business magnate,
investor, programmer,
inventor, philanthropist

William Henry Gates was born in Seattle, Washington state, USA. His father, also called Bill Gates, was a prominent lawyer and his mother was a banker and the daughter of a bank president; they had it in mind when Bill was young that he would become a lawyer. At the age of 13, he went to an exclusive preparatory school, Lakeside. The school's Mothers Club raised money to buy a computer terminal and a block of time on a General Electric computer, so that the students might get some computing experience.

The young Bill Gates showed an early interest in programming the General Electric system in BASIC and was released from Maths lessons in order to do this. He wrote his first computer program on this equipment, one that allowed users to play games with the computer. He was fascinated by the computer, in particular by the way it always carried things out perfectly: 'There was just something neat about the machine.' When the Mother Club computer time ran out, Gates and other students tried to get time on other systems.

One was a PDP-10 that belonged to Computer Center Corporation (CCC), who banned Gates and three other Lakeside boys for several weeks when it caught them exploiting bugs in the system to get free computer time. When the ban ended, the four boys offered to find bugs in the CCC software – in return for more computer time. Bill Gates was already showing considerable entrepreneurial ability. This relationship continued until 1970, when CCC went out of business, but the following year Information Sciences, Inc hired the four boys to write a payroll program. When the school realized Gates' abilities as a programmer, Lakeside hired him to construct the timetable that showed which students were in which classes. Gates altered the code so that he was always in classes where boys were outnumbered by girls!

In 1973, Bill Gates left Lakeside School, scoring 1590 out of 1600 on his SAT, and enrolled at Harvard, where he met Steve Ballmer who was eventually to succeed him as Chief Executive Officer of Microsoft. At Harvard, Gates did not have a well-defined plan of study, but spent a lot of time on the computers. He was still in touch with Paul Allen, a friend from Lakeside days.

When the MITS Altair 8800 was released in 1975, Gates and Allen saw an opportunity to launch their own software company, and Gates took leave of absence from Harvard to join Allen at MITS in Albuquerque, New Mexico. They set up an office in Albuquerque and called their partnership 'Micro-Soft', dropping the hyphen a year later. Gates, still only 20, was never to return to Harvard to complete his degree course.

"Be nice to nerds. Chances are you'll end up working for one."

Five years later, Gates and Allen licensed a computer operating system to IBM (International Business Machines) to use in the personal computer industry which was just then getting started. With the advent of the microchip it was suddenly possible to manufacture computers that were small enough to install in people's homes and offices. The computer system that Bill Gates and Paul Allen created, MS-DOS (Microsoft Disk Operating System), and all the applications systems that dovetail into it have been a phenomenal success. In November 1985, Gates launched the first retail version of Microsoft Windows.

From the earliest days onward, Gates and Allen have been motivated by the belief that the computer would be a valuable tool in every office and home. The Microsoft mission is to improve software continually, to make it easier, more cost-effective, and to make it more enjoyable for people to use computers. And the mission is successful.

Through his Microsoft firm, Gates has been able to maintain his remarkable dominance in the personal computer industry by producing repeated updates that are hugely successful in meeting customer needs and expectations – such as Windows 95, Windows 98, Windows Vista and Windows 7.

Microsoft became the world's largest producer of microcomputer software. Microsoft is now a huge multinational enterprise. It brought in revenues of almost 37 billion dollars in one year recently, and it employs 55,000 people in 85 countries. Adaptation to rapid change and keeping ahead of possible competitors are very important, and the level of investment is very high – over 6 billion dollars in one year.

Bill Gates is a very assertive and competitive businessman. He has made vigorous attempts to expand his business into new markets. One of these initiatives was his purchase in 1995 of the Bettmann Archives. This enabled him to transform historic photographs into digital images for use on-line as part of his Corbis resource, which is one of the largest resources of visual images in the world. In 1996 he made efforts to gain a big stake in the Internet market.

> *"Success is a lousy teacher.*
> *It seduces smart people into*
> *thinking they can't lose."*

By 1986, Bill Gates was a billionaire, and 10 years later a centi-billionaire. He is undoubtedly one of the richest people in the world; in 2010 he fell back to second place in the Forbes List, behind Carlos Slim; in 2011 he moved to fifth place. But he recently reminded some London schoolchildren, 'If I hadn't given my money away, I'd have more than anyone else on the planet. 99% of it will go.'

He is also, because through Microsoft he in effect controls the internet, one of the most powerful people in the world: his influence is incalculable. In 2006 he dropped out of the day-to-day running of Microsoft in order to focus on philanthropy, another great American tradition. He uses his money intelligently and thoughtfully. With his wife he set up the Bill and Melinda Gates Foundation, which another billionaire philanthropist, Warren Buffett, supports with huge donations. The Foundation sponsors global health and learning with an endowment that in 2009 stood at over 30 billion dollars.

As a computer expert, Gates always had an incredible eye for detail, and he extended this eye for detail to the running of his corporation. Yet side by side with this, he has shown unusual breadth of vision in his creation of what amounts to a world communication system.

"It's fine to celebrate success but it is more important to heed the lessons of failure."

ROBERT H. GODDARD

A Voyage to the Frontier of Space

QUOTE

"The dream of yesterday is the hope of today and the reality of tomorrow."

BIOGRAPHY

NAME:	Robert Hutchings Goddard	**NATIONALITY:**	American
BORN:	October 5, 1882 Worcester, Massachusetts, United States	**OCCUPATION:**	Professor, rocket scientist, physicist, inventor
DIED:	August 10, 1945 (Aged 62) Baltimore, Maryland, United States		

Robert Hutchings Goddard designed and built the world's first liquid-fuelled rocket, and successfully launched it in March 1926. It would be long after his death before it was recognized that the Space Age had begun. Born in 1882, Goddard first became interested in science when his father showed him how he could generate electrostatic sparks from the carpet: the five-year-old Robert was deeply impressed.

Later when Robert started experimenting, his father encouraged him by supplying a telescope, a microscope and a subscription to the magazine *Scientific American*. Robert was hooked on science, but especially with flight, at first with kites and balloons. From early on, he made diary notes on his work, a habit that was to prove very useful to him later; he even documented his failures in detail.

He was a thin, frail boy, usually in poor health, and two years behind his contemporaries in terms of schooling. He became a voracious reader perhaps because of this. He borrowed many books on science from the local public library.

Goddard's interest in interplanetary space travel dated from his reading of H. G. Wells' science fiction novel *The War of the Worlds* when he was 16 years old. At 17, he had a visionary experience while he was climbing a cherry tree to saw off dead branches. Up in the tree he was transfixed by the sky.

'As I looked toward the fields at the east, I imagined how wonderful it would be to make some device which had even the possibility of ascending to Mars, and how it would look on a small scale, if sent up from the meadow at my feet. It seemed to me then that a weight whirling around a horizontal shaft, moving more rapidly above than below, could furnish lift by virtue of the greater centrifugal force at the top of the path. I was a different boy when I descended the tree. Existence at last seemed very purposive.'

For the rest of his life, Goddard celebrated October 19 as Anniversary Day, the date of his rite of passage, the dawn of the idea of space travel.

His interest in flight led him to speculate about aerodynamics, and he started watching swallows and swifts, noting how they moved their wings and tails to control their flight. He wrote a paper about it, which was rejected for publication. Then he read Isaac Newton and decided to test Newton's Third Law of Motion in a stream, 'with devices suspended by rubber bands and devices on floats, and the said law was verified conclusively. It made me realize that if a way to navigate space were to be discovered, or invented, it would be the result of a knowledge of physics and mathematics.'

Goddard's health improved and he was able to go back to school, where he was hugely successful. He went on to the Worcester Polytechnic Institute, where he greatly impressed the Head of Physics, A. Wilmer Duff, who took him on as a lab assistant and tutor. Goddard was awarded a BSc in physics in 1908 and an MA in 1910. In 1912 he accepted a research fellowship at the Palmer Physical Laboratory at Princeton.

He first wrote about designing an efficient liquid-fuelled rocket in 1909. His first stated goal was to build a rocket which could be used to study the atmosphere. He was reluctant to admit that his ultimate goal was space travel, because most US scientists believed that this was unachievable.

Nor were the general public ready to treat such ideas seriously. Goddard tried to avoid interviews about his project, because he did not enjoy dealing with ridicule.

"Every vision is a joke until the first man accomplishes it; once realized, it becomes commonplace."

Early in 1913, Robert Goddard fell ill with tuberculosis. He had to leave Princeton and return to Worcester, where he slowly recovered. During his convalescence, he started spending an hour a day working on his rocketry notes. The time for thought made him realize that it was important to protect his ideas as intellectual property, and he began a series of patent applications. Of his total of 214 patents, two from the year 1914 in particular turned out to be milestones in the history of space flight; one patent was for a liquid-fuelled rocket, the other for a multi-stage rocket.

As his health improved in 1915, Goddard started planning his first rocket test. The first test launch was of a powder rocket, but he found that they only converted 2% of their fuel into thrust. He was eventually to achieve 50% efficiency with liquid fuel. He also ran an experiment to see whether a rocket would perform in a vacuum, as in interplanetary space. Contrary to other scientists' expectations, Goddard's experiment showed that rocket performance would improve in a vacuum.

By 1916, Goddard's experiments were costing more than he could afford out of a teaching salary. He looked for sponsorship and the Smithsonian was interested, asking him to elaborate. This was when Goddard produced his monograph, *A Method of Reaching Extreme Altitudes*. The Smithsonian agreed to support him for five years and Worcester Polytechnic offered a safe testing site at an abandoned Magnetics Lab.

In 1919, the Smithsonian Institution published Goddard's paper, which has since been seen as one of the pioneering works in rocket science. Goddard experimented with Laval's steam turbine nozzle, which had the effect of raising the efficiency of his rockets to 64%.

He had to deal with some harsh criticism in the press, as well as general ridicule, and he retreated from public discussion, even avoided discussion with colleagues if possible. This may have hampered his progress, as like any scientist he needed support and constructive criticism from other scientists. He got no support from the US government, but in 1929 he found a sponsor in Harry Guggenheim. The rocket experiments continued, now at Roswell in New Mexico. But the highest Goddard's rockets reached was 1.7 miles. It was a very long way from space flight.

Goddard's biggest failure was the low maximum altitude achieved. In 1937, planes were reaching heights of 10 miles and balloons 15 miles – and the German rockets performed better than Goddard's, who was convinced the Germans had pirated his design. But he was wrong – their design was different. When Goddard died in 1945, interplanetary travel must have seemed as far away as ever.

Goddard was, even so, a gifted engineer, an inspired theorist, a visionary. His work was to prove a major step towards space flight. His rockets had several sophisticated features, such as three-axis control, gyroscopes and steerable thrust, which meant that rockets could be steered while in flight.

In July 1969, the day after Apollo 11 was launched, *The New York Times* had the grace to offer an oblique and subtle posthumous apology to Goddard. After the dismissive 1920 editorial was summarized, it read, 'Further investigation and experimentation have confirmed the findings of Isaac Newton and it is now definitely established that a rocket can function in a vacuum as well as in an atmosphere. The Times regrets the error.'

"Just remember, when you think all is lost, the future remains."

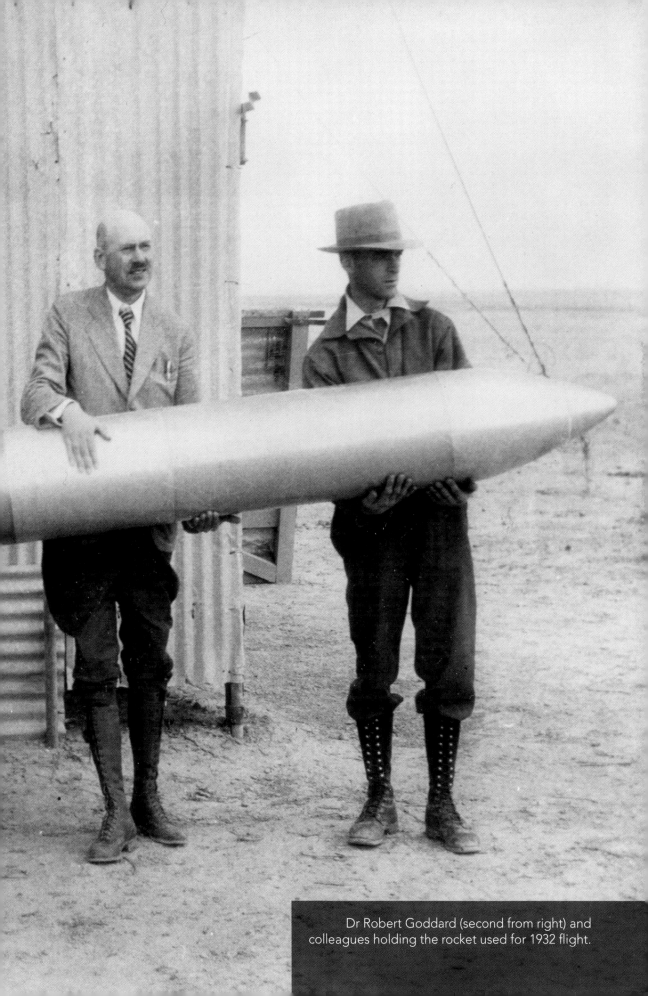

Dr Robert Goddard (second from right) and colleagues holding the rocket used for 1932 flight.

STEPHEN HAWKING

Black Holes, Dark Stars and the History of Time

QUOTE ━━━━━━━━━━━━━━━━━━━━━━━━━━━━━━━━━━━━━━━

"We are just an advanced breed of monkeys on a minor planet of a very average star. But we can understand the Universe. That makes us something very special."

BIOGRAPHY ━━━━━━━━━━━━━━━━━━━━━━━━━━━━━━━━━━━━━━━

NAME: Stephen William Hawking

BORN: January 8, 1942
Oxford, England,
United Kingdom

NATIONALITY: British

OCCUPATION: Theoretical physicist, cosmologist, Director of Research

Stephen Hawking is a cosmologist and theoretical physicist. He was Lucasian Professor of Mathematics at Cambridge for 30 years, retiring from the post in 2009. He is now Director of Research at the Centre for Theoretical Cosmology at Cambridge. He is well-known to the general public for his best-selling book *A Brief History of Time*, and also for his disability, resulting from motor neurone disease. He has made contributions in the fields of cosmology and quantum gravity, relating to black holes. He has provided, jointly with Roger Penrose, theorems about gravitational singularities. A singularity is a location where the gravitational field becomes infinite, as within a black hole.

Hawking's father was a London-based research biologist, but he and his wife Isobel decided to move to Oxford when she became pregnant. In late 1941, London was under constant German air attack and Oxford was seen as a safer place. After the war, the Hawking family moved to St Albans, where Stephen attended the High School for Girls (which received boys up to the age of 10). At 11, he went to St Albans School, where he was a good though unexceptional student. He still keeps in touch with the school. Originally, he wanted to study mathematics at university, but his father wanted him to apply to University College, Oxford, his own old college, and it happened that there was no mathematics fellow at University College at the time. Stephen therefore applied for a place there to read natural sciences instead, and won a scholarship.

He was already interested in relativity and quantum mechanics. His physics tutor, Robert Berman, commented later that Hawking could do things without looking to see how other people did them. 'He didn't have very many books, and he didn't take notes. Of course his mind was completely different from all his contemporaries.' His risky study habits put him on the borderline between a first and second class degree, but his *viva voce* examination made it clear to the examiners that he was cleverer than they were. After gaining his BA in 1962, he stayed on to study astronomy, until he found that the observatory at Oxford was only geared to observing sunspots, so he moved to Trinity Hall, Cambridge. There he started researching theoretical astronomy and cosmology.

Shortly after arriving at Cambridge, he started showing symptoms of motor neurone disease. Eventually he would lose almost all neuromuscular control. Two years later, after the disease had been stabilized, Hawking was able to resume work on his PhD project. In 1974 he accepted a visiting professorship at the California Institute of Technology in order to work with his friend Kip Thorne, a faculty member there. By this stage, though, he was unable to feed himself or get out of bed unaided; his speech was becoming slurred. He is now unable to speak at all. A device has been built to enable him to keyboard what he wants to say into a computer; a voice synthesizer then speaks the words. The distinctive robotic voice with its American accent became an integral part of Stephen Hawking's extraordinary persona.

In the late 1960s, Hawking worked with his friend Roger Penrose on a new mathematical model they created from Einstein's theory of relativity. This led on to Hawking proving many singularity theorems. These theorems provide a set of conditions under which a gravitational singularity in space-time could exist. What he was showing was that far from being rare mathematical curiosities, singularities are a generic feature of general relativity. He contributed to a mathematical proof that any black hole may be fully described by three properties – mass, angular momentum and electrical charge. With the same co-workers he proposed the four laws of black hole mechanics, and in 1974 calculated that a black hole should emit radiation, which has become known as Bekenstein-Hawking radiation – this emission should continue until the energy within the black hole is exhausted and the black hole evaporates.

> *"To confine our attention to terrestrial matters would be to limit the human spirit."*

There seemed to be no end to Hawking's new ideas. With Jim Hartle, he developed a model of the universe which has no boundary in space-time. This replaced the initial singularity of the classical Big Bang model. It was a revolutionary idea, that the universe is not closed – it has no end. Following on from this idea, in 2006 Hawking (with Thomas Hertog) proposed that the universe had no particular initial state and it is therefore not appropriate for us to formulate theories that 'predict' the current state of the universe from a presumed initial state. Instead he proposed a 'top-down' cosmology, which admits that the present layout of the universe allows for many possible histories. We inevitably search for and find the elements of the universe's history that allow matter and life; we select a history, and so we avoid the necessity of invoking a collection of multiple universes. And he has come up with many other revolutionary theories in various fields of physics, giving him a broad overview.

Many of the ideas are difficult for non-physicists to appreciate, and some seem closer to philosophy than to science, based as they are on reflection and speculation rather than observation and measurement.

His more populist pronouncements can make uncomfortable listening, some coming startlingly close to stating the obvious. Regarding extraterrestrial life, he believes that 'primitive life is very common and intelligent life is fairly rare' and 'the real challenge is to work out what aliens might actually be like'. 'If aliens visit us, the outcome would be much as when Columbus landed in America, which didn't turn out well for the Native Americans.' This is an idea that might have been lifted from H. G. Wells *The War of the Worlds*. In one interview, when he was asked about his IQ, Hawking came close to tying himself in a knot: 'People who boast about their IQ are losers … I hope I'm near the upper end of the range.' He famously introduced God on the closing page of *A Brief History of Time* – 'If we discover a complete theory, it would be the ultimate triumph of human reason – for then we should know the mind of God.' But subsequently he admitted that he did not believe in a personal God: 'the Universe can and will create itself from nothing.' So why did he mention God in his book?

To celebrate his 65th birthday in 2007, Hawking took a zero-gravity flight in preparation for a sub-orbital space flight in 2009; this was paid for by Sir Richard Branson. His zero-gravity flight was the first time in 40 years that he moved freely, out of his wheelchair, but his stated reason was 'to encourage public interest in space … I think the human race has no future if it doesn't go into space.'

Stephen Hawking is a very rare genius; he is a man who has a great many new ideas and greatly extends the scope of his academic discipline, but who also wants to interest the general public in the big ideas of science. To this end he is ready to appear in popular science fiction, playing himself in *Red Dwarf* and *Star Trek*. He has also become a symbolic figure to the world in his courageous struggle to overcome his profound disability – to go on working, to go on living, against the odds.

> *"I'm not afraid of death, but I'm in no hurry to die … I have so much I want to do first."*

MARTIN HEIDEGGER

The Simple Question of Being

QUOTE

"Tell me how you read and I'll tell you who you are."

BIOGRAPHY

NAME: Martin Heidegger

BORN: September 26, 1889
Meßkirch, Baden,
German Empire

DIED: May 26, 1976 (Aged 86)
Freiburg im Breisgau,
Baden-Württemberg,
Federal Republic of Germany

NATIONALITY: German

OCCUPATION: Philosopher

Martin Heidegger was born in 1889 in south-west Germany into a Catholic family, and when he was a boy he was prepared for the priesthood. In 1903 he went to the high school in Konstanz, where he was supported by a church-sponsored scholarship. In 1906, he moved to Freiburg, where his interest in philosophy was sparked by reading Franz Brentano's book, *On the Manifold Meaning of Being according to Aristotle*. In 1909, he became a Jesuit novice, but ill-health led to his discharge after only a few weeks. He entered Freiburg University to study theology, but left in 1911, terminating his training for the priesthood. Whether this was primarily because of his lack of spiritual vocation or because of ill-health is unclear.

He took up philosophy, mathematics and natural sciences, in 1913 completing a doctoral thesis on *The Doctrine of Judgement in Psychologism*. World War I might have brought everything to an end. He was conscripted into the army, but once again discharged after a few weeks on health grounds. Heidegger then worked towards gaining the chair of Catholic philosophy at Freiburg, by working on a further thesis, a requirement for teaching at the university. This thesis, *Duns Scotus's Doctrine of Categories and Meaning*, was completed in 1915. Then he was appointed lecturer and at first regarded himself as presenting a Catholic world-view, but he was very soon to switch from theology to philosophy.

He was, in 1918, once again conscripted and saw military service for the last 10 months of the war. He had by this time married a Protestant girl. Within a few weeks of returning to Freiburg, he formally broke with 'the system of Catholicism' and began lecturing in a new way, showing new insight. His lectures on phenomenology and his creative interpretations of Aristotle made him a landmark figure in philosophy. He had started as an assistant to Edmund Husserl, but became increasingly critical; he soon began a radical review of Husserl's views. On the other hand it is clear that Heidegger could not have achieved what he did without Husserl's work.

In 1923, Martin Heidegger became associate professor at Marburg University and the next five years were the most fruitful and successful of his career. His students were impressed by his originality and the intensity of his philosophical questioning. He expanded the scope of his lectures, teaching courses on time, logic and the history of philosophy. After publishing nothing for 11 years, which was a gap that threatened the future of his career, in 1927, he produced his most important work, *Being and Time*. It was recognized at once as a major work of 20th century philosophy. He was immediately made full professor at Marburg and a year later, when Husserl retired, full professor at Freiburg.

Heidegger's main interest was ontology, the study of being. In *Being and Time*, he tried to explore being by way of a phenomenological analysis of human existence. By phenomenology, Husserl and Heidegger both meant a descriptive and detached analysis of consciousness. Heidegger emphasized language as the vehicle by which the question of being can be explored. His exploration ranged widely, through ancient philosophy and also the more recent philosophy of Kant, Hegel and Nietzsche and the poetry of Hölderlin. He tried to pursue a line of thought that was no longer metaphysical, and became critical of the tradition of Western philosophy, because he thought it was nihilistic, obliterating the question of being. From just this summary, it is clear that Heidegger's writings are heavy weather; they are in fact notoriously difficult to read.

"Making itself intelligible is suicide for philosophy."

The major setback in Heidegger's career was his involvement in the Nazi movement, and this has prejudiced many against his philosophical works. Until Hitler's rise to power, Heidegger had been virtually non-political. But after Hitler was appointed chancellor of Germany in 1933, Heidegger became involved. He was elected rector of Freiburg University, which was a politically exposed position.

Interviewed by *Der Spiegel* in 1966 about this episode, Heidegger would claim that he was urged by his colleagues to present himself as a candidate, in order to prevent a Nazi party functionary from being appointed. It seems he also believed that he could influence the Nazi party, steer it in the right direction! In May 1933 he joined the party. During his term as rector he gave a number of speeches expressing support for Hitler and placed his high reputation as a scholar at the service of the party. Whatever his intention may have been, he was legitimizing the Nazi regime.

What is more surprising is that Heidegger resigned as rector just a year later, taking no further part in politics. His party membership was now a mere formality and he was regarded with suspicion by the Nazis; his freedom to publish and attend conferences was restricted. In his teaching, he inserted covert criticism of the Nazi regime and for a time he was under Gestapo surveillance. He was finally humiliated in 1944, when he was declared the most expendable member of the university faculty; he was sent to the Rhine to dig trenches.

When World War II ended, he was strongly criticized for showing Nazi sympathies in 1933–4 and he was forbidden to teach until 1949. He was dismissed from his chair of philosophy.

The 1930s were a period of philosophical turmoil for Heidegger. There was a change in his thinking known as 'the turn'. He became less systematic and more obscure, trying to find his way by exploring the texts of other philosophers, ancient and modern. He also explored poetry for ideas, leading to *What are Poets for?* (1946). His writings continued into the 1960s, when he produced *Time and Being* and *The End of Philosophy and the Task of Thinking*. He divided his time between his home in Freiburg, his second study in Meßkirch and a mountain hut in the Black Forest. But he was not cut off from the outside world completely. He was visited by friends, including the philosopher Hannah Arendt, the theologian Rudolf Bultmann and the physicist Werner Heisenberg – and he travelled widely. He remained intellectually active to the very end of his life.

Heidegger's 'mistake' of 1933 may have been a naive error of judgement, but he certainly paid for his mistake, suffering humiliating punishment at the hands of the post-war anti-Nazis for being a Nazi, just as he had suffered at the hands of the Nazis for his defection. It shows how difficult it is, even for a philosopher of Heidegger's brilliance, to know how to behave well in an evil society.

"The most thought-provoking thing in our thought-provoking time is that we are still not thinking."

GRACE HOPPER

A Pirate Dying to be Released

QUOTE

"Life was simple before World War II. After that, we had systems."

BIOGRAPHY

NAME: Grace Murray Hopper

BORN: December 9, 1906
New York City, New York,
United States

DIED: January 1, 1992 (Aged 85)
Arlington, Virginia,
United States

NATIONALITY: American

OCCUPATION: Computer scientist,
United States Navy Rear
Admiral

Grace Hopper, the pioneer computer scientist, was born as Grace Brewster Murray in 1906, in New York, the eldest of three children. When she was seven she decided to take alarm clocks to pieces to find out how they worked; her mother had to stop her after she had dismantled seven clocks. She was initially rejected by Vassar College because her Latin marks were too low, but was admitted at the age of 17. She gained a degree in mathematics and physics in 1928, and was awarded a Master's degree at Yale in 1930, then a PhD at Yale in 1934. Her doctoral thesis, *New Types of Irreducible Criteria*, was published the same year. Grace Murray became associate professor of mathematics at Vassar in 1941.

She was married to Vincent Hopper, a professor at New York University, until they divorced in 1945; she nevertheless kept her married name. In 1943 Grace Hopper was given leave of absence in order to join the US Navy Reserve, in spite of being underweight, nearly 7 kg (15 lbs) below the Navy minimum of 54 kg (119 lbs). Hopper came first in her class in 1944 and was assigned to the Bureau of Ships Computation Project at Harvard, with the rank of Lieutenant. There she worked on the computer programming staff led by Howard Aiken. Hopper and Aiken co-wrote three papers known as the Automatic Sequence Controlled Calculator.

When the war ended, Grace Hopper asked to be transferred to the regular Navy, but she was turned down because of her age; she was 38. She went on working in the Navy Reserve and remained at the Harvard Computation Lab until 1949. She preferred to turn down a full professorship at Vassar in order to continue working as a research fellow for the Navy at Harvard.

In 1949, she joined the Eckert-Mauchly Computer Corporation as a mathematician and was part of the team developing the UNIVAC I. After the company was taken over by Remington Rand, Grace Hopper became the company's first director of automatic programming and her department released some of the first programming languages, such as ARITH-MATIC, MATH-MATIC and FLOW-MATIC. A conference in 1959 brought together computer experts from government and industry. Hopper served as technical consultant to the committee, and several of her former employees served on the short-term committee that defined the new language, COBOL. This extended Hopper's FLOW-MATIC language with some ideas from IBM's COMTRAN.

"If it's a good idea, go ahead and do it. It's much easier to apologize than it is to get permission."

Grace Hopper believed that computer programs should be written in a language that was similar to English, not in a machine code, and COBOL was designed with that in view. COBOL went on to become the most successful business language in the world. At around that time, she was quoted as saying, 'To me programming is more than an important practical art. It is also a gigantic undertaking in the foundations of knowledge.'

She retired from the Naval Reserve at the end of 1966 with the rank of Commander. She was recalled to the Navy in 1967, where she served as director of the US Navy Programming Languages Group. She retired again in 1971 but was again recalled to active duty in 1972. She was promoted to the rank of Captain in 1973. She developed software relating to the COBOL program – for the entire Navy. After some television coverage of her career, some lobbying led to her promotion to Commodore by special Presidential appointment. In 1985 this was revised to Rear Admiral. She was compulsorily retired the following year, just four months short of her 80th birthday. A celebration was held aboard the US Navy's oldest commissioned ship, the 189-year-old USS *Constitution*.

She commented that people still didn't understand the nature of her work, 'I handed my passport to the immigration officer, and he looked at it and looked at me and said, *What are you?*' Yet still Grace Hopper went on working. She was a senior consultant to Digital Equipment Corporation, and she lectured widely on the early days of computers. A memorable part of her talks was her illustration of a nanosecond. She cut an old Bell telephone cable into 30 cm lengths and handed them to her audience. That was the maximum distance light travels in one nanosecond in a vacuum.

Grace Hopper was an unusual pioneering computer scientist, one of the first programmers of the Harvard Mark I computer. She encouraged others to innovate too. She said, 'A ship in port is safe; but that is not what ships are built for. Sail out to sea and do new things.' She developed the first compiler for a computer programming language. She also popularized and perhaps invented the term 'debugging' for fixing glitches, a term that originated with the removal of a real-life moth from a Harvard Mark I computer. The moth itself has been preserved as an exhibit at the Smithsonian Institution.

She was, naturally, sometimes referred to as 'Amazing Grace' and had a destroyer named after her, USS *Hopper*. She was well known for her lively and irreverent speaking style, as well as a rich treasury of early war stories. She also received the nickname 'Grandma COBOL'. Jay Elliot, who was at Apple with Steve Jobs during the 1980s, described Grace Hopper as being 'all Navy, but when you reach inside, you find a pirate dying to be released'.

"You don't manage people, you manage things. You lead people."

EDWIN HUBBLE

Measuring the Milky Way

QUOTE

"Past time is finite, future time is infinite."

BIOGRAPHY

NAME:	Edwin Powell Hubble	**NATIONALITY:**	American
BORN:	November 20, 1889 Marshfield, Missouri, United States	**OCCUPATION:**	Astronomist, cosmologist
DIED:	September 28, 1953 (Aged 63) San Marino, California, United States		

Edwin Hubble, the astronomer son of an insurance executive, was born in Missouri, USA in 1889. When he was 11, the family moved to Wheaton, Illinois. At school in Wheaton, Hubble was noted more for athletic than academic prowess. He did not seem to be a boy with intellectual interests, though he went on to study mathematics, astronomy and philosophy at the University of Chicago, where he gained a BSc in 1910. Then he spent three years in England at Oxford University as a Rhodes Scholar. He studied law, fulfilling a promise extorted by his dying father, and was awarded a Master's degree. During this stay he acquired faux-British mannerisms and dress, which he doggedly maintained when he returned to America, to the irritation of some of his American colleagues.

Back in the USA, Hubble found work at the New Albany High School in Indiana, teaching physics, mathematics and Spanish – and coaching basketball. After a year of this he went back to astronomy at Chicago, where he was awarded a PhD in 1917 for Photographic Investigations of Faint Nebulae. He would, after all, not keep his promise to his father to become a lawyer.

Hubble arrived at Mount Wilson in California in 1919, just as the 100-inch Hooker Telescope was completed, then the biggest telescope in the world. The prevailing view among astronomers up to that moment was that the universe consisted entirely and exclusively of our own galaxy, the Milky Way. But the new telescope enabled Hubble to see more. His 1922–23 observations of several spiral nebulae, including the Andromeda Nebula, proved that these were of the order of a million light-years away, too far away to be part of the Milky Way, and that they were in fact galaxies in their own right. The idea had been proposed before and opposed by many well-established astronomers, including Harlow Shapley. Shapley had measured the diameter of the Milky Way, and estimated 300,000 light-years. This huge diameter was 10 times the previously accepted figure, and Shapley still believed that the whole universe was contained within that enlarged galaxy.

Hubble had his findings published, first in *The New York Times* and then in a paper presented to the American Astronomical Society. Hubble's revelation fundamentally altered the prevailing view of the universe. The universe did not, after all, consist of a single galaxy, but many galaxies spread an enormous distance apart from each other. He devised a system for classifying galaxies, according to their appearance on photographic images; this became known as the Hubble sequence.

Hubble plotted his measurements of galaxy distances against Vesto Slipher's and Milton Humason's measurements of the redshifts associated with those galaxies. He discovered that there was a directly proportional relationship between the two; the further away the galaxy, the more exaggerated its redshift. This Redshift Distance Law of galaxies is now referred to as Hubble's Law. There was considerable variation or scatter within the data set, but he was able to plot a trend line from the 46 galaxies. From this he inferred a value for the Hubble Constant of 160km/sec/million light-years.

> *"I knew that even if I were second or third rate, it was astronomy that mattered."*

This is much higher than the value that is generally agreed today, but Hubble was working from the restricted data that was available to him then. His incorrect figures caused problems because they implied that our galaxy was far larger than other nearby galaxies. In 1932, Hubble's figure for the constant was roundly criticized in print. It was not until the 1950s that the source of the mistake was realized. Hubble's analysis did not allow for variations in galaxy brightness; there are changes in luminosity that are due to the evolutionary stage of the galaxy. The value Hubble calculated for his constant was wrong.

Hubble's Law (1929) states that the greater the distance between any two galaxies, the greater their relative speed of separation. If the redshift is interpreted as a measure of recession speed, it is consistent with the solutions of Einstein's equations of general relativity for a homogeneous expanding space. The concept of an expanding universe already existed, but the publication of Hubble and Humason's evidence led to a wider acceptance of the idea of an expanding universe. But perhaps Hubble has been given too much credit for this.

Two years earlier, in 1927, a Belgian physicist, Georges Lemaître, published a paper showing that data collected by Hubble and two other astronomers was then already sufficient to show a velocity-distance relationship between galaxies, and moreover that this supported a model of an expanding universe based on Einstein's general relativity equations. Had Hubble seen Lemaître's paper?

In the 1930s, Hubble was plotting the distribution of galaxies and the curvature of space. His data led him to conclude that the universe was flat and uniform, but there was a deviation from flatness at large redshifts. In other words, things changed towards the edge of the universe.

Hubble thought that his data gave a more reasonable result if the redshift correction was made assuming no recession, and he maintained this position to the end of his career, apparently trying to keep open the option that no true expansion exists. Hubble was ready to see redshift as representing 'a hitherto unrecognized principle of nature'. Perhaps he couldn't believe where his evidence was leading him.

But Einstein had had a similar failure of nerve, when his calculations had led him to a very strange place. In 1917, Einstein saw that his new theory of general relativity showed that the universe must be either contracting or expanding. It was too disturbing, too incredible, to be true. To escape from the 'truth' of his calculations, Einstein added a cosmological constant. When he heard of Hubble's discovery he said changing his equations was 'the biggest blunder of my life'.

Hubble's two major contributions to knowledge were the confirmation that galaxies other than the Milky Way existed and the redshift in the light spectra from other galaxies increased with increasing distance from the Earth (Hubble's Law), though Lemaître has a prior claim that has not been sufficiently recognized. These two findings were to have enormous implications for the model of the expanding universe that emerged in the early 20th century.

Questions hang over Edwin Hubble's originality and primacy, which reduce the claims that can be made on his behalf. How brilliant was he? He certainly brought some key ideas about the universe to the fore. Hubble spent a lot of time in his later life trying to establish the status of astronomy as a branch of physics, but this was merely so that he could qualify as a candidate for the Nobel Prize in Physics. He wanted a Nobel Prize, even hiring a publicity agent to promote his cause. The Prize Committee decided after Hubble's death that astronomy was indeed eligible, but then it was too late: the Nobel Prize cannot be awarded posthumously.

"Equipped with his five senses, man explores the universe around him and calls the adventure Science."

NASA Hubble Space Telescope image showing the giant galaxy cluster Abell 1689, containing about 1,000 galaxies and trillions of stars.

ALI JAVAN

Standing on the Shoulders of Giants

QUOTE

"Listen closely as those around you speak; great truths are revealed in jest."

BIOGRAPHY

NAME: Ali Mortimer Javan

BORN: December 26, 1926
Tehran, Iran

NATIONALITY: Iranian American

OCCUPATION: Physicist, inventor

Ali Mortimer Javan is an Iranian-American physicist and inventor based at MIT. He remembers, as a child, playing with a lot of gadgets. 'My first attempt to invent something was for an idea that could never have worked out. Conceptually, it was impossible. But I tried anyway. I was seven or eight at the time.' His parents were Azeris from Tabriz and he was born in Tehran. Studying first at Alborz High School, he went on to Tehran University. After the end of World War II, Javan emigrated to the USA, completing his PhD in physics at Columbia University in 1954.

In 1955, Ali Javan began working as an assistant at the Radiation Laboratory with Charles Townes, who had been his research supervisor. Together they worked on the atomic clock and used the microwave atom beam to study the structure of atoms such as thalium and copper.

He joined the Bell Telephone Laboratories in 1958, shortly after working out the principle of a gas discharge helium neon laser device. He predicted the eventual significance of this device. In 1961, Javan joined the Massachusetts Institute of Technology as an associate professor of physics, and in 1964 he became professor emeritus of physics at MIT.

In 1960 he was responsible, with William R. Bennett, for inventing the gas laser, his principal claim to fame. A gas laser is a laser in which an electric current is passed through a gas to produce light. The gas laser was the earliest continuous-light laser to be based on the principle of converting electrical energy to a laser light output. The US patent which Bennett and Javan took out described the device as the 'gas optical maser'.

It was first tested in December 1960. Javan has described the first time laser beam transmission was used to conduct a telephone conversation; 'I put in a call to the lab. One of the team members answered and asked me to hold the line for a moment. Then I heard a voice [the voice of Mr Balik], somewhat quivering in transmission, telling me that it was the laser light speaking to me.'

He recently reflected on his discovery that, in the world of science, it is often said that when the time comes for an invention or a discovery to be made, if you don't do it, someone else will. 'But it is not always the case. People can miss a good idea. When it comes to the laser – my kind of laser, the gas laser – I'm convinced it could have been invented in the 1930s, not 30 years later. Physicists had come very close to the idea of lasers by 1937. From the literature you can see that they were just about to grasp the idea but then moved away from it. Had I been around in the 1930s, I'm sure I would have invented it then.' We can only speculate how the laser might have been used in World War II. Perhaps radar would have been laser radar, not microwave radar.

Javan mentions that Newton admitted that he had only been able to make his discoveries about gravitation thanks to the work of other people before him; he was standing on the shoulders of giants. Javan is conscious that his invention depended on research work done by other scientists in the 1920s on the wave nature of atoms. 'There were giants at that time who made these early discoveries – Neils Bohr, Schrodinger, Einstein … '

"I don't wish to be everything to everyone, but I would like to be something to someone."

But Ali Javan is also insistent that his invention had much to do with his own persistence. 'It's difficult to pinpoint the moment when a creative idea is born. At some moment you know everything about your invention even though you're not aware that you do. And then suddenly it all fits together and the discovery is made. When I came up with the idea for the gas laser, much of it, if not all, was based on my intense involvement in the work I was doing. But I knew I could make the laser work; otherwise, I wouldn't have gone after it.'

The significance of this invention is enormous because of its many applications. Javan and Bennett's gas laser marked the beginning of fibre optic communication. Laser telecommunication by way of fibre optics is the key technology used in the internet. Helium-neon gas lasers were the first to be mass-produced, and are now part of our everyday lives.

Every time we pass through a supermarket checkout, we see the bright light of a device that reads the barcode on the products we are buying; these checkout scanners operate using a device based on Javan's laser invention. The invention is all around us, often invisible, operating DVD players and laser printers. Javan's original invention has been largely supplanted by a second-generation laser invention, the diode-pumped solid state lasers. Javan's device is nevertheless still in use for specialized applications such as holography, due to the long coherence length of its laser beams.

For his invention, Javan has received many awards, including the Albert Einstein World Award of Science in 1993.

Ali Javan keeps the original laser device, the one-metre-long grandfather machine that he and Bennett built in 1960, in his office; Javan calls it 'Adam'. The Smithsonian Institution would, understandably, like to acquire it. Javan has not rested on his laurels. He is a man who emanates concentration, energy, determination and perseverance. 'From the very beginning people who knew of my idea were very skeptical. Even people on my own team who were working on it with me had hesitations and doubts. Over the years I've seen this tendency in a lot of people. Even good physicists are sometimes insecure in their own beliefs; they waver with uncertainty.' But Javan knew his machine would work.

He is still as active as ever, pushing the boundaries of technology for the benefit of mankind.

"Some of the most beautiful days come completely by chance. But even the most beautiful days eventually have their sunset."

STEVE JOBS

Let's Go Invent Tomorrow

QUOTE

"Focus and simplicity – that's been one of my mantras."

BIOGRAPHY

NAME: Steven Paul Jobs

BORN: February 24, 1955
San Francisco, California,
United States

DIED: October 5, 2011 (Aged 56)
Palo Alto, California,
United States

NATIONALITY: American

OCCUPATION: Entrepreneur, marketeer,
inventor

The charismatic pioneer of personal computers, Steve Jobs, was born in San Francisco in 1955. His parents were unmarried university students and Steve was adopted at birth by Paul and Clara Jobs. Steve was always emphatic that Paul and Clara were his parents, '1000%'. Clara was a payroll clerk for one of the high-tech companies in what was to become Silicon Valley. Paul was a machinist for a company that manufactured lasers and naturally taught his son basic electronics – and how to work with his hands. So each of Steve Jobs' adoptive parents had contact with areas where he would achieve great things: an example of nurture over nature, perhaps.

Steve went to Homestead High School in Cupertino, California. After school, he attended lectures at the Hewlett-Packard Company in Palo Alto, later working there with Steve Wozniak as a summer employee. Jobs went on in 1972 to Reed College at Portland in Oregon. He dropped out after one term, but continued attending classes at Reed while his friends at the college let him sleep on the floor in their rooms. He went to the local Hare Krishna temple to get free meals. One of the courses he attended in this unusual way was a calligraphy course and he later said that if had not dropped in on that course 'the Mac would have never had multiple typefaces or proportionally spaced fonts'.

In 1974, Jobs went to work as a technician at Atari. He also travelled to India with a friend from Reed College to visit Neem Karoli Baba, in a quest for spiritual enlightenment. When they reached Neem Karoli Baba's ashram they found it virtually deserted: he had died almost a year before. Jobs nevertheless stayed in India for some months, experimenting with LSD before returning, head shaved and wearing Indian clothing. He practised Zen Buddhism, going on long retreats for meditation. This 'countercultural' strand was a very important part of the way he was to think and work.

When Jobs went back to Atari, who assigned him the task of making a circuit board for a computer game, and offered $100 for each chip eliminated. Jobs was not interested enough to do this, and sub-contracted the work to Wozniak; they would split the fee. This was an indication of Jobs'

entrepreneurial spirit. Atari were surprised when Wozniak came up with a solution that eliminated 50 chips. They gave Jobs $5,000. He told Wozniak, Atari had only given him $700 and Wozniak's share was only $350. When he owned up 10 years later, Jobs justified this deception by saying he needed the money.

Jobs greatly admired Edwin Land, the inventor of instant photography and founder of Polaroid, and consciously based his own career on Land's. In 1976, Steve Jobs, Steve Wozniak and Ronald Wayne founded Apple Computers in the garage of the suburban Los Altos bungalow that was the Jobs' family home. Wayne dropped out fairly early, leaving Jobs and Wozniak as the main co-founders of the company. The purpose in setting up Apple as a company was to sell the Apple I computer that Wozniak had invented. Two years later, Apple took on Mike Scott to act as its Chief Executive Officer. The early years of Apple were turbulent. In 1983, Jobs lured John Sculley away from Pepsi-Cola to be a replacement CEO; 'Do you want to sell sugar water for the rest of your life, or do you want to come with me and change the world?' he asked Sculley.

"Design is not just what it looks like and feels like. Design is how it works."

Jobs showed brilliant insight in seeing the commercial potential of Xerox's mouse-driven graphical user interface. This led to the creation of the Apple Lisa. Shortly after that, an Apple employee called Jef Raskin invented the Macintosh. Jobs understood that his company had something very special to offer, and he introduced the Macintosh to a very enthusiastic annual shareholders meeting in January 1984.

He was a brilliantly persuasive presenter, though his employees from that time remember him as erratic and temperamental as a manager, running meetings that went on until midnight. He was a demanding perfectionist. Relations between Jobs and Sculley worsened, turning into a power struggle. Jobs discovered that Sculley was trying to organize a coup and in May 1985 called a board meeting to resolve the issue. The Apple board sided with Sculley and Jobs was in effect forced to resign.

Steve Jobs set up a new company, NeXT, shortly afterwards. He said 20 years later that being fired from Apple was a relief; it enabled him to be creative again. 'It was awful-tasting medicine, but I guess the patient needed it.'

In 1986, he acquired the computer graphics section of Lucasfilm Ltd, which became Pixar Animation Studios. This is how in 1995 he was credited in the film *Toy Story* as an executive producer. He stayed CEO and major shareholder until The Walt Disney Company acquired it in 2006; this made Jobs Disney's biggest individual shareholder, with 7% of Disney's shares, and a Disney director. Another unexpected development, in 1996, was Apple's acquisition of NeXT, a deal that meant Jobs was once again part of the company he had co-founded. His role now was adviser, and in this role he oversaw the development of the iMac, iTunes, iPod, iPhone and iPad.

Steve Jobs' astonishing business career was brought to a premature end by pancreatic cancer, from which he died at the age of 56. He was a great salesman, and he was both admired and criticized for his rare skills at persuasion and selling. He was unquestionably a brilliant presenter and a man with a keen eye for new technology that had great commercial potential.

He especially liked an old Wayne Gretzky quote: 'I skate to where the puck is going to be, not where it has been', and he added, 'We've always tried to do that at Apple. Since the very, very beginning. And we always will.' He was above all a remarkably able entrepreneur in a great American tradition, opportunistic, and with more than a streak of ruthlessness, ready to make money out of other people's inventions. His net wealth the year before he died was estimated at 8.3 billion dollars.

But it is possible that we are dazzled by his enormous wealth and his charismatic presentations, which were to an extent self-presentations. We may in the process have undervalued the co-founder of Apple, Stephen Wozniak. It was Wozniak, after all, who was the actual creator of the original Apple computer – its hardware, operating system and circuit board design. Wozniak was the real inventor. Wozniak's net wealth in 2010 was estimated at 100 million dollars. This makes him appear to be less successful commercially than Jobs, though still far more successful than most of us – but in terms of brilliance of mind and technical creativity, there is a good case for regarding Wozniak as the real wizard behind Apple. But Steve Jobs had the know-how to make it all happen.

"Being the richest man in the cemetery doesn't matter to me ... Going to bed at night saying we've done something wonderful ... that's what matters to me."

JAMES JOYCE

On the Brink of Madness

QUOTE

"I care not if I live but a day and a night, so long as my deeds live after me."

BIOGRAPHY

NAME: James Augustine Aloysius
Joyce

BORN: February 2, 1882
Rathgar, Dublin, Ireland

DIED: January 13, 1941 (Aged 58)
Zürich, Switzerland

NATIONALITY: British

OCCUPATION: Author

The writer James Joyce was born in Dublin in 1882, the eldest of the 12 children of John and Mary Joyce. John Joyce was a rate collector for Dublin Corporation. In 1891, John Joyce became bankrupt and was suspended from his job; two years later he lost the job completely, which began the family's slide from gentility into poverty. John Joyce drank heavily and was hopeless with money. The young James Joyce went to Jesuit schools, but at the age of 16, he rebelled against Catholicism and this rebellion seems to have spilled over into his approach to literature shortly afterwards. Joyce studied English, French and Italian at University College Dublin in 1898, and became active in Dublin's literary and dramatic circles. His very first publication was a review of Ibsen, and he had a note of thanks for this from Ibsen himself – a promising beginning.

After graduating in 1903, Joyce went to Paris to study medicine, but gave it up because of the difficulty of taking in an extensive technical vocabulary in a foreign language. He appealed to his parents for financial support which they could not give. Then a telegram arrived, with a prophetically Joycean spelling mistake: '*NOTHER DYING COME HOME FATHER*'. Joyce's mother had cancer. She made a last-ditch attempt to get her son to make confession and take communion. The family knelt in prayer at her bedside, but James and his brother Stanislaus refused to join in.

He met a chambermaid called Nora Barnacle, with whom he eloped to Europe. They first went to Zürich, then Trieste, in search of a post teaching English. Eventually he got a job in Pola, in what is now Croatia, teaching English to Austro-Hungarian officers. This ended in 1905, when a spy ring was discovered in Pola and all aliens were expelled. Joyce moved back to Trieste.

In 1909, he went back to Dublin with his son George, partly to see his father, partly to arrange for the publication of *Dubliners*. While there he launched the first cinema in Ireland, the Volta Cinematograph, using money from Italian backers. The idea was to find a way of making money. The cinema venture was initially successful, but failed when Joyce returned to Trieste. In 1912, Joyce was back in Dublin again to try again to get his publisher, George Roberts, to publish *Dubliners*. Again he failed: it was an ongoing battle. He never again returned to

Dublin, in spite of pleas from his father and the poet W. B. Yeats.

Another problem that beset Joyce was with his eyes. In the end he needed more than a dozen operations on them. Meanwhile the money problems continued.

In World War I, most of Joyce's students were conscripted, and he moved back to Zürich, where he met Frank Budgen, who became an important friend and literary adviser. He also met, through Ezra Pound, Harriet Shaw Weaver, who became Joyce's patron. Over the next 25 years she supplied him with an income that released him from teaching and enabled him to concentrate on writing. In Zürich, he wrote *Exiles* and started work on *Ulysses*. Zürich suited him well, but after four years the nomad in him had the urge to move back to Trieste again.

> *"Think you're escaping and run into yourself. Longest way round is the shortest way home."*

In 1920, Ezra Pound invited him to Paris for a week, and he stayed for 20 years. He finished *Ulysses* and found he was establishing a reputation as a modernist writer. Joyce's daughter Lucia was thought by the family to be suffering from schizophrenia and they took her to the great psycho-analyst C. G. Jung. Later, when Jung read *Ulysses*, he came to the conclusion that Joyce himself had schizophrenia. Jung said Lucia and her father were both headed for

James Joyce with publishers Sylvia Beach and Adrienne Monnier at Shakespeare & Co bookshop, Paris, 1920.

the bottom of a river; the difference was that Lucia was falling and Joyce was diving.

In Paris, Joyce was nursed through the years when he was writing *Finnegans Wake* by Eugene and Maria Jolas. Probably without their support and Harriet Weaver Shaw's financial help Joyce's books would never have been completed. The Jolases published a literary magazine called *Transition*. In it, they published sections of *Finnegans Wake* under the neutral title *Work in Progress*. When the Germans invaded France in 1940, Joyce fled back to Zürich. In 1941 he suddenly suffered a perforated ulcer and died.

Ulysses appeared in 1922, the same year as Eliot's *The Waste Land*, two landmarks in the history of modern English literature. Joyce used a variety of techniques to present his characters, including stream of consciousness, jokes and parody. The action takes place on a single day in Dublin in 1904, and is a kind of satire on Homer's *Odyssey*. Odysseus becomes Leopold Bloom, Penelope becomes Molly Bloom and Telemachus becomes Stephen Dedalus. The monotony and squalor of everyday life in Dublin is a far cry from the dazzling epic of Homer. The book also contains a strangely detailed portrait of the city, and Joyce went to a great deal of trouble, using a 1904 directory, to make sure he got residents and their addresses right. The formal structure of the book is unusual, with chapters associated with particular colours, arts, sciences and bodily organs, and this formality contrasts with the kaleidoscopic writing line by line. It is a ground-breaking piece of writing, and on a grand scale.

Finnegans Wake is a similar, large-scale piece of avant-garde writing. He had completed the first two parts of the book by 1926, but was then slowed up by the death of his father, the mental illness of his daughter, and his own eye problems. Luckily he was given strong support by younger writers like Samuel Beckett. But Joyce was beset by weird psychological fixations. One of these was the idea that he could hand over the completion of the book to his friend James Stephens. His reason was that Stephens was born in the same hospital as Joyce, exactly one week later, and shared Joyce's first name. It was an unhelpful piece of superstition.

Reaction to the surreal writing in *Finnegans Wake* was naturally mixed. There were negative reactions from Joyce's brother Stanislaus and Ezra Pound. In his book *The Mask of Sanity*, the writer and doctor Hervey Cleckley described *Finnegans Wake* as 'a 628-page collection of erudite gibberish indistinguishable to most people from the familiar word salad produced by hebephrenic patients on the back wards of any state hospital'. This was not so very far from Jung's view of *Ulysses* ('fathomless').

Joyce's great and wholly innovative work abandons all conventions of character construction and narrative. It is also written in a very peculiar language, as if several European languages and cultures have been exploded and the pieces allowed to reassemble wherever they fall. Some passages, where words and phrases are transformed repeatedly, and the puns multiply, are very funny. Somehow, from the spray of words, a new and surreal world appears. Joyce seems sometimes to be looking back towards Laurence Sterne and Lewis Carroll, sometimes forward to ITMA, *The Goon Show* and *Monty Python*. Those who dislike *Finnegans Wake* have described it with a phrase from Joyce himself, as the 'usylessly unreadable Blue Book of Eccles'.

Joyce had the level of heedless daring and the irrepressible inventiveness that we expect of a genius. Perhaps he was mad as well; his writing does seem to teeter on the brink of madness.

> *"I've put in so many enigmas and puzzles that it will keep the professors busy for centuries arguing over what I meant, and that's the only way of insuring one's immortality."*

PERCY JULIAN

The Science of Prejudice and Fire-Bombs

QUOTE ━━

"I would forever fight to keep hope alive."

BIOGRAPHY ━━━━━━━━━━━━━━━━━━━━━━━━━━━━━━━━━━━━━

NAME: Percy Lavon Julian

BORN: April 11, 1899
Montgomery, Alabama,
United States

DIED: April 19, 1975 (Aged 76)
Waukegan, Illinois,
United States

NATIONALITY: American

OCCUPATION: Research chemist, medical
professional, civil rights
activist

The African-American research chemist Percy Lavon Julian was born in Montgomery, Alabama in 1899. His mother Elizabeth was a schoolteacher and his father was a post office clerk. At that time it was very rare for black American children to be fully educated, but Percy Julian's parents were committed to getting all their children into higher education. It is often the case that very high achievers have a background of very strong parental support – and the supply of confidence that goes with that.

Julian went to DePauw University in Greencastle, Indiana, where he found himself in a small minority of African-American students. Greencastle had a policy of racial segregation, so he was not allowed to sleep in the college dormitories. He initially stayed at a boarding-house off-campus, but even there he was refused meals. It took some days for him to find a place where he could both sleep and eat, a fraternity house, where he was allowed to sleep in the attic in return for stoking the boiler. In spite of these humiliations, Julian graduated and his father moved the whole family to Greencastle so that Julian's siblings could also attend college there.

Julian wanted to do research for a doctorate in chemistry, but was given to understand that this would not be easy because of his race. He became a chemistry instructor at Fisk University, then won a scholarship to continue his chemistry studies for an MSc degree at Harvard. But the only way forward was to study abroad, and Julian was given a fellowship that allowed him to study in Vienna, where he was awarded his PhD in 1931.

In Europe he experienced a freedom from the racial prejudice that had been so oppressive in America; there was irony in this, as far worse racial prejudice was about to overwhelm central Europe when the Nazis took power. But his experience in Vienna was a good one. He was able to join in freely in seminars, social gatherings, the theatre, and found total acceptance among his intellectual peers.

On his return to the USA, Julian suffered a new setback. He started teaching at Howard University, where he unwisely antagonized

two co-workers, Jacob Shohan and Robert Thompson. They retaliated by publishing Julian's racy and sexually indiscreet letters from Vienna. During the summer of 1932, these letters appeared in the press and Julian was forced to resign.

He was saved by an offer from William Blanchard to return to DePauw University to teach organic chemistry. Together with another student from Vienna, Josef Pikl, Julian synthesized the natural plant product physostigmine. This was to be the line of research where he became extremely successful – pioneering work in the chemical synthesis of medicinal drugs from plants. But racism remained a problem: as a black man, in 1936, he could not hold a professorship at DePauw. Julian wrote to the Glidden Company, asking for a 5-gallon sample of its soybean oil to use as a base for the synthesis of human steroidal sex hormones. W. J. O'Brien, vice-president at Glidden, phoned Julian offering him the post of director of research at Glidden's Soya Products Division in Chicago.

An attraction for O'Brien was that Glidden was buying a solvent plant from Germany and Julian was a fluent German-speaker. When Julian arrived in Chicago in 1936 he oversaw the assembly of the new plant. Then he designed and constructed the world's first factory for the production of industrial-grade soy protein; this product could replace more expensive milk-based products in industrial processes such as coating and sizing paper, glue for making plywood and the manufacture of water-based paint. A by-product of Julian's work in this area was the fire-fighting foam that was adopted by the US Navy to quell oil and petrol (gasoline) fires aboard ships. This saved the lives of thousands of sailors, especially in World War II.

Percy Julian's research took a new direction in 1940 when, still at Glidden, he began synthesizing progesterone, oestrogen and testosterone from plant chemicals that he was able to isolate from soybean oil by means of a foam technique that he invented. Sex hormones had until then been hard to reproduce in anything but very small quantities, but Julian was finding a way of producing them in significantly larger volumes. Now, for the first time, the female hormone progesterone was on the American market in bulk. The mass production of other sex hormones followed soon after. The significance was that it became, in the 1940s, possible to treat hormonal deficiencies more cheaply. Product patents held by European pharmaceutical companies meant that high prices for sex hormones were protected. Julian and his co-workers were driven to take out patents on Glidden's behalf, to protect the key processes for preparing hormones from soybean.

Another major area where Percy Julian worked was in cortisone. In 1949, Philip Hench at the Mayo Clinic announced that he had found cortisone to have a dramatic effect in the treatment of rheumatoid arthritis. Cortisone was currently being produced by using a complicated synthesis, in 36 steps; it was very expensive, partly because it entailed using osmium tetroxide, an expensive chemical. Within five months, Percy Julian announced that he had developed an improved process in cortisone production, one that eliminated the need for osmium tetroxide. By 1950, he was producing related drugs that had some of the effect of cortisone.

In 1953, Glidden made the decision to pull out of steroid production which, in spite of Julian's work, was fairly unprofitable. This prompted Julian to resign from Glidden, giving up a huge salary (almost $50,000 a year). He set up his own company, Julian Laboratories, Inc, in Franklin Park, Illinois. At the same time, Julian moved with his family from Chicago to Oak Park, a village where the Julians were the first black family. Here again they encountered racial prejudice; their home was fire-bombed before they moved in and dynamited a year later. These attacks electrified the community into supporting the Julians and a community group was set up to help them. But the house had to be defended with a shotgun.

In business too, Julian found that he had to defend himself against huge odds. He repeatedly found that he was up against very large and powerful companies bent on excluding competition. He sold Julian Laboratories in 1961 for $2.3 million. Three years later he founded Julian Associates and Julian Research Institute.

Recognition of his key role as a pioneer in the synthesis of medicinal drugs came in 1973, when this grandson of a slave was elected to the National Academy of Sciences. Two years later, Percy Julian died of liver cancer. The American Chemical Society declared Percy Julian's synthesis of physostigmine as one of the 25 greatest achievements in the history of American chemistry.

"I feel that my own good country robbed me of the chance for some of the great experiences that I would have liked to live through."

CARL JUNG

Knowing Your Own Darkness

QUOTE

"Everything that irritates us about others can lead us to an understanding of ourselves."

BIOGRAPHY

NAME: Carl Gustav Jung

BORN: July 26, 1875
Kesswil, Thurgau, Switzerland

DIED: June 6, 1961 (Aged 85)
Küsnacht, Zürich, Switzerland

NATIONALITY: Swiss

OCCUPATION: Psychologist, psychiatrist, psychotherapist

The psychologist Carl Jung, born in 1875, was the son of a stern and tyrannical clergyman who often quarrelled openly with his wife, Carl's mother. The cold and arid home environment drove him deeper and deeper into himself. He invented solitary games. The tension within the family intensified when the parents started sleeping apart. Mental disturbances generated vivid dreams that he would recall and analyze later in life.

He studied medicine in Basel and then continued his psychology studies in Paris under Pierre Janet. He worked as a physician under Eugen Bleuler at the Burghölzli mental clinic in Zürich from 1900 until 1909, and lectured in psychology at the University of Zürich from 1905 to 1913. Jung was a staggeringly prolific writer, and one of his early publications was *Studies in Word Association*, in which he invented the term 'complex'. He also wrote *The Psychology of Dementia Praecox* (now called schizophrenia). These publications led directly to a meeting with Sigmund Freud in Vienna in 1907. Along the way he acquired a wealthy wife, a marriage that made his life much more comfortable. He also met and made friends with Albert Einstein.

Jung became Sigmund Freud's leading disciple and collaborator. But Jung was a researcher with an independent mind, and he followed his own original lines of thought. The moment Jung set out his new ideas on the libido and the unconscious, in 1912, there was tension as Freud felt his authority challenged. Jung became increasingly critical of Freud's insistence on the psychosexual origins of neuroses; to Jung this insistence on the sexual was too doctrinaire.

Jung substituted his own term, libido, for a general non-specific life-force, while Freud remained fixed on the sexual drive as the root of most psychological problems. They regularly exchanged dreams and analyzed them. When, one day, Freud refused to tell Jung one of his dreams 'because it would undermine my authority', Jung knew that it was time for him to go his own way and in 1913 he parted company with Freud. Jung felt that Freud lacked a philosophical background; Jung himself was immersed in philosophy. He also saw that Freud made a mistake in restricting analysis to the personal. We are all steeped in history and zeitgeist; the way our parents treat us and the way we are educated are historical, not personal.

There was an exchange of over-heated, over-emotional letters. The two great psychologists were struggling to understand their own minds and emotions, and unable to understand the strength of their effect on one another. It was like a tiff between teenage lovers.

Jung and Freud had exchanged dreams and psychoanalyzed one another. Jung knew a lot about the workings of Freud's mind which even in his final years he was not prepared to divulge. He smiled and said, 'There's such a thing as a professional secret.'

> *"Knowing your own darkness is the best method for dealing with the darknesses of other people."*

A Freudian bystander might have judged that Freud was playing the father, and Jung was reacting badly to this as he had not enjoyed his relationship with his father, so he was playing the ultra-rebellious son. One tyrant-father was quite enough. Probably this is what their colleague Ernest Jones thought, as he watched this personal and professional tragedy unfold.

The two founders of modern psychology went their separate ways. Possibly as a result of this loss, Jung had a serious mental breakdown which lasted – significantly – for the duration of World War I. Jung even made the extraordinary suggestion that the external struggle was a projection of his own breakdown. And that was part of his insanity. He went on seeing patients during this period; one wonders whether he can have helped them much. One patient he diagnosed as being in the final stages of syphilis and gave him only weeks to live. The patient wisely sought a second opinion; he turned out to be manic-depressive and lived for another 50 years.

In later life, Jung admitted that he nearly lost his reason between 1913 and 1918. He fell back on repeating to himself, 'I have a diploma from a Swiss university, I have a wife and five children, I live at 228 Seestrasse, Kusnacht.' Nietzsche had gone through a similar ordeal and drowned in his inner world. Jung managed to use his knowledge of the unconscious mind to swim through it and turn the episode into a rebirth.

From 1920, his composure recovered, but he needed a special retreat. He chose a peaceful lakeside site at Bollingen, where he built a tower-refuge, its architecture heavy with personal symbolism. Personal mystification of this kind was important to Jung. It was essential, for everybody, to connect with the mythic world, and confront the archetypes.

Jung founded his own school of analytical psychology in Zürich. What Jung shared with Freud was a profound belief in the fundamental importance of dreams as a window onto the unconscious mind. Where they differed was in the interpretation of dreams. Freud delved until he found the sexual metaphor and was then satisfied that he reached the dream's meaning. Jung saw that the sexual content of a dream might be no more than metaphorical language; still deeper layers might lie beneath. Where Freud stopped, Jung went on digging.

After World War II ended, Jung was invited to give a lecture 'explaining' the war. He developed the idea that the German people have a tendency to be dominated by a particular archetype, which he called Wotan, the great Teutonic god of war. Hitler, he argued, was a witch-doctor who had worked the German people up to a pitch where the Wotan archetype had taken over the entire nation. It was a characteristically

daring view of the world – one that no-one before Jung could possibly have considered.

Jung's most controversial idea was the collective unconscious. People are born with a set of archetypes (basic images and situations) which they then recognize in the outside world and respond to accordingly. This extraordinary idea implies that some kind of memory transcends death and that certain images and situations in our minds are ancestral. Another controversial idea is synchronicity; the idea that thematically related events can sometimes happen close together without any causal relationship.

That capacity to produce entirely new and remarkable ideas – and hundreds of them – is what makes Jung unquestionably a genius. In old age, he cultivated his own archetypal image of the Wise Old Man – an éminence grise. He was a vain old man and cared what the world thought about him. But it was professionalism more than vanity that made him answer all his correspondence personally. Some correspondents were fans, some were crying for help. He answered them all.

"The meeting of two personalities is like the contact of two chemical substances; if there is any reaction, both are transformed."

JOHN MAYNARD KEYNES

Money Makes the World Go Round

QUOTE ━━━━━━━━━━━━━━━━━━━━━━━━━━━━━━━━━━━━━━

"The long run is a misleading guide to current affairs. In the long run we are all dead."

BIOGRAPHY ━━━━━━━━━━━━━━━━━━━━━━━━━━━━━━━━━━

NAME: John Maynard Keynes

BORN: June 5, 1883
Cambridge, Cambridgeshire,
England, United Kingdom

DIED: April 21, 1946 (Aged 62)
Firle, East Sussex, England,
United Kingdom

NATIONALITY: British

OCCUPATION: Economist

Keynes was born in 1883 into an upper-middle-class family in Cambridge, England. His mother Florence was a local social reformer and his father, John Neville Keynes, was an economist and lecturer in moral sciences at Cambridge. They were strongly supportive and loving parents, who kept the same family home all their lives and the children were always welcomed back.

After Eton, Keynes studied mathematics at King's College, Cambridge. He was a member of the semi-secret Cambridge Apostles, an exclusive club reserved for the most intelligent students. In common with other members, he kept his bond with the Apostles intermittently for the rest of his life. He also became President of the Cambridge University Liberal Club. He graduated in 1904, staying on for another year to study under Alfred Marshall and Arthur Pigou. Keynes developed their ideas on the quantitative theory of money, eventually writing *A Tract on Monetary Reform*.

In 1906, Keynes took a post in the British Civil Service, at the India Office. He took advantage of this position to gather material for his first economics book, *Indian Currency and Finance*, which describes the way India's monetary system worked. By 1908 he was already bored with the India Office and returned to Cambridge University to work on probability theory. This rather odd venture was privately funded by his father and by his old teacher, the economist Arthur Pigou. In 1909, he accepted a University lectureship in economics, this time funded personally by another don, Alfred Marshall.

His earnings rose as he took on pupils for private tuition and when he was elected a fellow of the University. Then in 1911, he became editor of the *Economic Journal*. After the publication of his *Indian Currency* book in 1913, he was seen by the British government as an economics expert, and one who would be particularly useful in the unstable conditions during World War I. Keynes did not formally re-join the Civil Service when war broke out, but travelled to London 'on request' to work for the Treasury. He quickly ascended through the bureaucracy, so that by 1919 he was the Treasury's financial representative at the Versailles peace conference at the end of the war. He resigned, knowing that the reparations demanded by the Allies were excessively punitive, too great a burden to put on the German economy.

His objections to the Versailles Treaty turned him into a celebrity, when they were published in 1919 as *The Economic Consequences of the Peace*. 'The amounts demanded by the Allies were so large', he wrote, 'that a Germany that tried to pay them would be crippled by poverty and therefore become dangerously unstable.'

The book's economic analysis was penetrating and damning – and proved correct by subsequent events. It also contained an insightful analysis of the allied members who made up the peace committee – the Council of Four: Georges Clemenceau, David Lloyd George, Woodrow Wilson and Vittorio Orlando: 'The Council of Four paid no attention to these issues [including making Germany and Austro-Hungary into good neighbours], being preoccupied with others – Clemenceau to crush the economic life of his enemy, Lloyd George to do a deal and bring home something which would pass muster for a week, the President [Wilson] to do nothing that was not just and right.'

> *"Capitalism is the astounding belief that the most wicked of men will do the most wicked of things for the greatest good of everyone."*

When he was back teaching at Cambridge again, he became a notable speaker and journalist, and a member of the Bloomsbury Group. In the 1920s he was an advocate of the quantity theory of money, which is now called monetarism, writing *Tract on Monetary Reform* and *Treatise on Money*.

His main theme was that an economy can be stabilized by stabilizing prices, and to stabilize prices a government's central bank needs to lower interest rates when prices rise and raise them when prices fall.

But Keynes' view seriously changed when unemployment began to increase dramatically. This made him explore other factors, leading him to write *The General Theory of Employment, Interest and Money*. This book was a revolution in economic thought, including the major new concept of 'aggregate demand' as the total sum of consumption, investment and government spending. In the book, Keynes also expounded the theory that full employment could only be sustained with the aid of government spending.

Economists are still divided about what Keynes believed was the cause of high unemployment. Some have thought it might be persistent high wages, but in *General Theory* Keynes argued for wages being kept stable. A general cut in wages would reduce income, consumption and aggregate demand, so any 'gain' from a lower price of labour would be offset. Keynes thought government should show initiative by mounting public works projects and hiring the unemployed.

There was some opposition to Keynes's conclusion, but the idea took hold in the USA, where the government set up public works projects. Keynes was an advocate, even so, of free markets. He believed that once full employment had been achieved, the market mechanism could be allowed to operate freely.

As the end of World War II approached, in 1944, the Bretton Woods Conference was held. It was at this conference that the International Monetary Fund was set up. Keynes was a key contributor at this conference and was one of the architects of the post-war system of fixed exchange rates.

Keynes died of a heart attack at his farmhouse at Tilton near the village of Firle, deep in the countryside of East Sussex near Brighton, England in April 1946. He was 62, and he was survived by his wife and both of his parents.

Keynes's ideas on economics were so influential in the middle of the 20th century that his name was applied to an entire school of modern thinking about the subject. Some of his ideas were truly revolutionary, many were controversial. The phrase 'Keynesian economics' has become a kind of benchmark according to which most economists coming afterwards can be defined. Yet little of Keynes's original work survives in modern economic theory. His ideas have been revised, expanded and modified by various economists. Today's version of Keynesian economics may have its roots in Keynes's *General Theory*, but it is largely the work of later economists. A new branch of economics, called econometrics, was created in order to explore and explain Keynes's macroeconomic models.

The original Keynesian models may have been superseded, but they led the way to a raft of new ideas from a new generation of economists. He remains a huge influence on economic thinking, and on Western politics. In particular he overturned the classical economic model which held that free markets will provide full employment so long as workers are flexible in their wage demands. In other words, he demonstrated that imposing low wages on the labour force is not the answer. This idea led on to Western capitalist governments adopting a principle of social liberalism.

In the 1970s, Milton Friedman and other economists criticized Keynesian economics, expressing doubts about the ability of governments to regulate business cycles. But the onset of the current global financial crisis in 2007 led to a startling revival of Keynesian thought. Not surprisingly, *Time* magazine has listed Keynes as one of the 100 most important and influential people of the 20th century.

When the accumulation of wealth is no longer of high social importance, there will be great changes in the code of morals.

D. H. LAWRENCE

The Burning Desire for Love

"I can never decide whether my dreams are the result of my thoughts, or my thoughts the result of my dreams."

BIOGRAPHY

NAME: David Herbert Lawrence

BORN: September 11, 1885
Eastwood, Nottinghamshire,
England, United Kingdom

DIED: March 2, 1930 (Aged 44)
Vence, France

NATIONALITY: British

OCCUPATION: Writer, literary critic,
painter

David Herbert Lawrence was born in Eastwood, Nottinghamshire, England in 1885. He was a trail-blazing English novelist whose father was a barely literate coal-miner. Educated at Nottingham High School and then University College, Nottingham, it was his mother who nurtured his scholarly and literary side, and it was through her encouragement that he became a schoolteacher and writer. In the early days, Edward Garnett, a publisher's reader, noticed and praised his work, which gave him confidence; Edward's son, David Garnett, also befriended Lawrence.

After the success of his first novel, *The White Peacock,* published in 1911, Lawrence made the premature decision to make his living by writing, and it was already obvious to some critics that a young writer of great force and originality had arrived. The following year he eloped with Frieda von Richthofen, a cousin of the German flying ace. She was, more to the point, already married, and was the wife of Ernest Weekley, a professor at Nottingham University.

The runaway lovers toured Germany, Austria and Italy for a year and then, after Frieda's divorce from Ernest, married in 1914. By this time, Lawrence had made a substantial reputation for himself with his second novel, *Sons and Lovers*. The couple returned to England just as World War I with Germany broke out. They lived in a cottage in Cornwall, surrounded by local suspicion as the German woman was regarded with fear and hatred.

In 1915, Lawrence published *The Rainbow*, and was surprised and alarmed to find that he was the target of a prosecution for obscenity. This brush with the law stopped Lawrence in his tracks for a while. When the war ended, he left England for Italy, where he wrote some travel impressions, *Twilight in Italy*, and another novel which adventurously explored sex and marriage, *Women in Love*.

He settled in Mexico, but he suffered from tuberculosis and a worsening of his condition drove him to return to Europe to live in Italy. His novel *Lady Chatterley's Lover*, covering the same controversial territory as before, was published privately in Florence in 1928. Once again he was prosecuted for obscenity. *Lady Chatterley's Lover* was not published in Britain until after a landmark obscenity trial in 1961.

> *"I like to write when I feel spiteful. It is like having a good sneeze."*

Lawrence was by all accounts a poor painter, but in the maelstrom that was modern art in the first three decades of the 20th century it was difficult for many to tell the difference between good art and bad. Lawrence mounted an exhibition of his sexually explicit paintings in London in 1929, and was apparently surprised to be accused once again of obscenity.

Lawrence died of tuberculosis near Nice in March 1930. The obituaries that followed his death were generally unsympathetic or hostile. An exception was E. M. Forster's obituary, which described Lawrence as 'the greatest imaginative novelist of our generation'. Later, the influential critic F. R. Leavis praised his artistic integrity and moral seriousness. The body of work he achieved was remarkable, not least because of his physical frailty; he was gradually overwhelmed by tuberculosis, an extremely debilitating disease, and had two serious bouts of pneumonia along the way.

Few doubt that the paintings are poor, and only hold any interest because it was Lawrence who painted them, but readers and literary critics are divided about Lawrence's novels. His writing, especially in the descriptive passages, is wonderful, however, some of his melodramatic dialogue has suffered from too many inferior copies and satirical recreations over the years which have now rendered the original unintentionally comedic. His poetry has generally escaped the scorn of sarcastic comedy routines and the critics, and contains many beautiful observations of natural scenery. His collected poems were published in 1928.

> *"I want to live my life so that my nights are not full of regrets."*

Lawrence's novels are highly original and had a profound influence on other writers of his own and subsequent generations. It was Lawrence who opened the marital bedroom door and made it permissible for novelists to explore what happened behind it. Lawrence also challenged other writers to deal more honestly and less sentimentally about sexual feelings and emotions, about the emotional differences between men and women, about the sexual problems that result from those differences, about the emotional strains that exist between the generations within families. Above all, Lawrence expressed and analyzed sex as a motive force for human action. Lawrence's novels were an inevitable outcome of Freud's revelations. The lid was off sexuality, and that changed the 20th century.

Lawrence's exposé of sexual relationships and what he saw as the need for spontaneity in relationships nevertheless feature as part of a larger picture. Overall, what Lawrence was seeking to do was to reflect on the dehumanizing effects of the lives that people were compelled to lead in the fall-out of the Industrial Revolution. In this, he was strongly influenced by growing up in Nottingham, in the middle of a huge coalfield, as the son of a poorly educated coal-miner. He felt the negative effects of industrialization very directly.

Lawrence was original, challenging and controversial. Some people deeply hated what he was doing – and some still hate him for it. However, others idolized him. He was one of the most powerful and distinctive of modern English novelists, producing three of the most influential novels of the 20th century: *The Rainbow*, *Sons and Lovers* and *Women in Love*.

"Be still when you have nothing to say; when genuine passion moves you, say what you've got to say, and say it hot."

LE CORBUSIER

The Spatial Awareness of Light

BIOGRAPHY ━━━━━━━━━━━━━━━━━━━━━━━━━━━━━━━━━━━━━━━

NAME: Charles-Édouard Jeanneret-Gris

BORN: October 6, 1887
La Chaux-de-Fonds,
Switzerland

DIED: August 27, 1965 (Aged 77)
Roquebrune-Cap-Martin,
France

NATIONALITY: Swiss / French (from 1930)

OCCUPATION: Architect, designer,
painter, urban planner,
writer

While many people have heard of the great French architect Le Corbusier, few have heard of Charles-Édouard Jeanneret-Gris, which was his real name. Part of Jeanneret's brilliance lay in establishing his public persona of Le Corbusier – and hiding behind it. He was born in 1887, at La Chaux-de-Fonds near Neuchâtel in Switzerland.

Designing his first house at the early age of 17, Jeanneret then studied for a short time in Paris with the architect Auguste Perret, who was a pioneer in the use of reinforced concrete for the construction of buildings. In 1910, he went to work with Peter Behrens in Germany. A cosmopolitan pattern in his life would find expression in a similarly cosmopolitan architectural style, a style not rooted in any particular place or tradition, a pure and disembodied modernist style which could successfully be built anywhere in the world. In 1916, Jeanneret settled in Paris, where for some years he worked at industrial research and as a painter; some of his architecture shows the influence of the Cubist style invented by Pablo Picasso.

In 1919, with Amédée Ozenfant, he published the Purist manifesto. Jeanneret, adopting the pseudonym Le Corbusier (The Engineer), started to work on a new theory of architecture. In this he established relationships between the forms seen in machinery and the techniques and shapes of modern architecture. He affirmed engineer-building as the only approach appropriate, both economically and spiritually, to the 20th century.

His position was a logical outcome of the long process of the Industrial Revolution, which had the effect of taking people out of their traditional rural environment and making them into city-dwellers. Instead of making their living from the land, they worked in factories; people lived with, and from, machines. 'Style is a lie,' Le Corbusier said. 'The house is a habitable machine.' He had become not just a great practitioner of architecture, but a great doctrinaire theorist too.

He held up the exact engineering fitness of the steamship's shape to its function: it was a perfect model for the land architect.

The simple lines and shapes that came with reinforced concrete perfectly expressed a building's function. His buildings would always look stripped, minimalist, windswept and bleak. It is a style that lends itself particularly well to the strong sunlight and sharply defined shadows of the Mediterranean.

In 1923, he published his book, *Vers une Architecture*, where he outlined his architectural theories. This book and two others produced later, *Le Modulor* in 1948 and *Le Modulor 2* in 1955, had a worldwide impact on both building design and city design in the 20th century. The *Modulor* was a system using units of standard size, the proportions of which depended on the proportions of the human figure. He was concentrating on the means of building construction, which needed to be on an industrial scale, hence the use of mass-produced modules. Even window frames and built-in furniture were to be mass-produced.

"Architecture is the learned game, correct and magnificent, of forms assembled in the light."

The first building Le Corbusier designed was the *Unité d'Habitation* in Marseilles, a huge housing unit designed as a self-contained community in 1945–50. The complex was conceived as a cluster of tall buildings. When the overall scheme, the Radial City, was built the cluster of tall buildings would form a pattern sticking up from a carpet of low-rise buildings and open spaces. That was the vision. This arrangement was Le Corbusier's preferred town-planning concept. He used it again in his design for Chandigarh, the new capital city of the Punjab.

One of Le Corbusier's best-known buildings is the *Pavillon de l'Esprit Nouveau,* designed for the Paris Exhibition of 1925. He was also a member of the ten-man team responsible for designing the United Nations Building in New York in 1950.

Le Corbusier liked to give his buildings flat roofs. This was partly to give them a clean, cubic appearance, and partly to enable him to install a roof garden – a feature he particularly liked. Thick concrete slabs laid on sand, with open, grass-grown joints, insulate the house beneath and reduce the reaction of the concrete structure to varying weather conditions.

Another distinctive feature of Le Corbusier's buildings is his use of pilotis, or piers, steel reinforced concrete pillars raising the building off the ground so that people or vehicles can pass underneath. Le Corbusier invented the piloti and used it first in his design for the *Cité Universitaire* in Paris. Now, of course, we see them everywhere. He believed in designing not just buildings, but entire cities for them to stand in. He similarly believed in designing furniture that would harmonize with the new designs for buildings. In the 1920s, he designed furniture – chairs especially – in collaboration with Charlotte Perriand. He used tubular metal in their construction – another major innovation which is now commonplace.

Le Corbusier's futuristic designs also hovered in the minds of many European architects when they designed housing to replace the low-rise buildings destroyed in World War II. His idea of the 'City in the Sky' was the basis for many of the high-rise apartments that were seen as the post-war way forward. But as a master architect, Le Corbusier would never have approved the cheap materials and shoddy workmanship used in the 1950s and 60s, that cut corners and turned the new tower blocks into a living nightmare for their occupants.

Many features of modern furniture, modern buildings and modern cities that we take for granted these days were originally devised by Le Corbusier. And, although the buildings of his many imitators may be inadequate replicas of the great man's architectural vision, ultimately, there can be little debate over Le Corbusier's originality, genius or legacy.

"The business of architecture is to establish emotional relationships by means of raw materials."

Notre Dame du Haut Chapel by
Le Corbusier, Ronchamp, France.

JAMES LOVELOCK

Civilization Hasn't Got Long ...

QUOTE

"Geological change usually takes thousands of years to happen but we are seeing the climate changing not just in our lifetimes but also year by year."

BIOGRAPHY

NAME: James Ephraim Lovelock

BORN: July 26, 1919
Letchworth, Hertfordshire,
England, United Kingdom

NATIONALITY: British

OCCUPATION: Scientist, environmentalist,
futurologist

The independent scientist, environmentalist and predictor of the future, James Lovelock, was born in Letchworth in Hertfordshire, England in 1919. His parents were working-class people who strongly believed in education. His father, Tom Lovelock, was illiterate until he went to technical college, and his mother, Nell, started work at 13 in a pickle factory. The Lovelocks moved to London, where he attended Strand School; the young James was unhappy there as he hated authority. He was unable to afford to go to university. He believes that this had the virtue of stopping him from becoming too specialized, and that it later helped him in forming the Gaia hypothesis.

James Lovelock attended evening classes at Birkbeck College and then did two years (which was all he could afford) of a degree course in chemistry at Manchester University. His status as a student qualified him for temporary deferment of military service in World War II, but he also registered as a conscientious objector. Later he relinquished his objection in the light of Nazi atrocities, and tried to enlist, but was turned down because his medical research was considered too valuable. In 1948 he gained a PhD in medicine.

James Lovelock invented many scientific instruments, some designed for NASA's interplanetary exploration program. The instruments designed in the 1960s were for the analysis of extraterrestrial atmospheres and planetary surfaces. It was while working for NASA that he developed his Gaia hypothesis, which portrays the earth (or at least its biosphere) as a self-regulating and self-protecting entity, functioning like a single large organism.

The Viking program in the 1970s was intended to establish whether there was life on Mars, and many of the sensors and experiments were designed to resolve this question. This prompted Lovelock's interest in the Martian atmosphere, which was found to be in a stable state with little oxygen, methane or hydrogen and a huge amount of carbon dioxide, a stark contrast with the Earth's atmosphere. Even before the Viking probes were launched, it seemed to Lovelock unlikely that the Martian atmosphere would support life.

Lovelock went on to develop the electron capture detector, which helped to establish the persistence of CFCs and their role in depleting ozone in the Earth's stratosphere. He studied the earth's sulphur cycle and helped to develop the CLAW hypothesis, a mechanism by which the Earth's climate system might in theory be controlled biologically.

In 1974, Lovelock was elected a Fellow of the Royal Society in London, and has been awarded many prizes for his innovative work, including the Geological Society's Wollaston Medal in 2006. He became a Companion of Honour in 2003.

> *"Sadly, it's much easier to create a desert than a forest."*

It was James Lovelock who was the first to detect the widespread presence of CFCs in the Earth's atmosphere. At first, he thought they constituted 'no conceivable hazard', not realizing that the chlorine they released would attack the ozone layer; that link was discovered by Sherwood Roland and Mario Molina in 1974, for which Roland and Molina were awarded the 1995 Nobel Prize in Chemistry.

Lovelock's idea that the atmosphere and biosphere of the Earth together form a complex interacting system was named Gaia, after an ancient earth-goddess, at the suggestion of the novelist William Golding. The key idea is that the biosphere acts as a regulator which enables the atmosphere to continue to sustain life. The Gaia hypothesis has gained acceptance among many environmentalists, but it has not gained wide acceptance among scientists. The main challenge is the question, 'How can natural selection acting on individual organisms lead to the evolution of planet-wide stability?' Lovelock responded to such criticism with a model called Daisyworld, which purports to show how individual and low-level effects can translate up to a planetary-scale stability.

In recent years, Lovelock has to an extent broken faith with his own Gaia model, expressing fear about the threat from global warming caused by the alleged man-made greenhouse effect. If the Earth's atmosphere and the organisms living in it (*human beings included*) are part of a self-regulating system, why should we be afraid of inflicting damage on that system? There is a logical inconsistency here. In 2004, Lovelock spread further alarm among his environmentalist supporters by expressing support for nuclear power. 'Only nuclear power can now halt global warming.' In 2005 he said, 'I am Green, and I entreat my friends in the movement to drop their wrong-headed objection to nuclear energy.'

But he believed that nuclear energy was a good thing as far back as the 1980s, when he said, 'I have never regarded nuclear radiation or nuclear power as anything other than a normal and inevitable part of the environment. Our forebears evolved on a planet-sized lump of fall-out from a star-sized nuclear explosion, a supernova that synthesized the elements that go to make our planet and ourselves.'

Lovelock's 2006 book, *The Revenge of Gaia* argues that the human race's lack of respect for Gaia has damaged the system to a level where the planet may not be able to recover. He cites the destruction of the rain-forests, the reduction in biodiversity, and man-made global warming as major challenges to Gaia's ability to regulate itself. While his arguments may or may not be valid both in general and in detail, they do show a lack of respect for, a lack of confidence in, his original concept of Gaia – the very idea for which he became famous.

In a more recent book, *The Vanishing Face of Gaia* (2009), and in press interviews, Lovelock has become even more pessimistic, predicting that within 90 years, 80 percent of the human race will have perished, and the current change in climate will last 100,000 years. *The Vanishing Face* goes so far as to reject any scientific arguments that disagree with the evidence (which he prefers) that sea levels are rising. At this point his arguments lose objectivity.

Data on worldwide sea level comes from two sources, measurements of the ocean surface taken from satellites and measurements taken on shorelines by tidal gauges, and the evidence from the two sources conflicts. The satellite data shows that sea level is rising globally, while many of the tidal gauges show that sea level was rising until 1998 but subsequently stabilized or fell slightly. Possibly the satellites are measuring the decay of their own orbits, not the oceans rising.

The truth is that the alleged movements in the ocean surface lie at the limits of instrumental accuracy – but instrumental accuracy is just the area of James Lovelock's expertise, so one might have expected him to be less dogmatic and more circumspect about the sea level evidence. At the moment Gaia looks like a brilliant idea betrayed by its own originator. Only time will tell whether the younger Lovelock or the older Lovelock is right.

"We are the intelligent elite among animal life on Earth, and whatever our mistakes, Earth needs us."

NELSON MANDELA

A Magical Inspiration to the World

BIOGRAPHY ━━━━━━━━━━━━━━━━━━━━━━━━━━━━━━━━━━━━━━

NAME: Nelson Rolihlahla Mandela

BORN: July 18, 1918
Mvezo, South Africa

DIED: December 5, 2013 (Aged 95)
Johannesburg, South Africa

NATIONALITY: South African

OCCUPATION: President of South Africa (1994 – 99), anti-apartheid activist and politician

The charismatic South African leader, Nelson Rolihlahla Mandela, was born in the Transkei, South Africa in 1918, where he was a member of the royal family of the Tembu tribe. Mandela became a successful lawyer in Johannesburg, where he set up the first black legal practice in South Africa. Then, in 1944, when he was 26, his political career began and he joined the African National Congress.

For the next 20 years, Mandela directed a campaign of defiance against the South African government, in protest against its racist policies. In May 1961, he organized a three-day national strike. The police tried to head it off with mass arrests of black activists, and altogether over 10,000 black people were detained. The police wanted to arrest Mandela, but when they called at his home in Orlando, near Johannesburg, he was out. His wife Winnie answered the door and asked them for the search warrant; they didn't have one. When they returned with a warrant, they searched the house and found nothing, and Mandela became known as the Black Pimpernel for his skill at evading arrest.

But he was eventually caught and brought to trial in October 1962. Specifically he was accused of being the mastermind behind the call for a national strike. He pleaded not guilty. A few weeks later the court found him guilty and imprisoned him for five years for incitement.

With the failure of the national strike, Nelson Mandela despaired of using non-violent means of overturning the racist regime. He turned instead to violence and helped to found the Spear of the Nation movement. Inevitably, the South African authorities retaliated, re-arresting Mandela and putting him on trial for more serious crimes. While Mandela was in prison, the police raided the ANC's underground headquarters, where they discovered Mandela's diaries, which contained notes on guerrilla warfare. In April 1964, he went on trial for treason. He was accused of sabotage and trying to overthrow the South African government by revolution. Mandela bravely told the court in Pretoria that his purpose was to rid the country of white domination. 'I do not deny that I planned sabotage. We had either to accept inferiority or fight against it by violence.'

Mandela was a trained lawyer, and he was able to marshal a spirited and coherent denial. His memorable testimony, given in June 1964, lasted four hours. But his eloquence was in vain. He was sentenced to life imprisonment. The police tried to smuggle Mandela and eight other convicted men out of the courthouse without anyone noticing. But the crowd spotted Mandela and ran along the street shouting, 'We have the strength!'

He was flown from Pretoria to Cape Town, then ferried by boat out to the penal colony on Robben Island. Although (just) within sight of the mainland, it has a strong current of cold Antarctic water sweeping past it, and escape was impossible.

Nelson Mandela continued to be a political force while in prison. He became a potent symbol of the subjugation of the black population of South Africa; he became a rallying-point. The symbolism of Mandela's captivity became a worldwide phenomenon, and a coordinated international campaign for his release was launched. His imprisonment became an increasing embarrassment to the South African government. When thousands of cards flooded in to mark Mandela's 60th birthday, the authorities refused to let him have them, but the point had been very effectively made; the world had by no means forgotten Nelson Mandela.

"The greatest glory in living lies not in never falling, but in rising every time we fall."

Winnie Mandela, Nelson Mandela's controversial wife, was also frequently subjected to restrictions, so that her freedom of action was curtailed. In May 1987, she was invited to speak on her husband's behalf by the liberal white students of Witwatersrand University of Johannesburg. The police moving in to stop the speech, resorted to whips, tear gas and 120 arrests in order to silence her.

Alongside the campaign to release Mandela, there was a worldwide campaign for the South African government to end its system of apartheid, the anti-black racial discrimination that saturated every aspect of South African life. Economic sanctions were applied, with many countries refusing to trade with South Africa. For a long time these sanctions had little effect, and the white South Africans seemed set to maintain their privileged position for ever, but suddenly in the 1980s sanctions began to bite.

President F. W. de Klerk took office in 1989 and introduced liberalizing measures that started the process of dismantling apartheid. Within months of being elected, President de Klerk visited Mandela in prison, preparing him for freedom and the new role he was about to play. The ban on the ANC was lifted, restrictions on political meetings were removed.

Nelson Mandela was released from captivity in February 1990, on de Klerk's orders. There was worldwide rejoicing. At the age of 71, Mandela was free. At the same time the white supremacy within the South African government crumbled. The whole country was on the brink of a massive political and cultural transformation. Mandela was made president of the ANC, and he opened negotiations with de Klerk about the future of the country. Cleverly, at the same time he pressed other countries to continue applying pressure; apartheid had to be abolished completely. In 1993, Mandela and de Klerk were jointly awarded the Nobel Peace Prize for their work on the process of reform, and the following year Mandela became South Africa's first black president.

Many feared that a bloodbath would follow, as old scores against the white community were settled by newly-empowered blacks. Mandela was the natural figurehead for the newly emergent black South Africa, and it would have been understandable if he had used his new-found power to punish, humiliate or even destroy his ex-gaolers. In fact, Mandela showed incredible restraint and magnanimity, encouraging people to confess and come to terms with the bad events of the past, but without undue recrimination, without revenge.

Mandela won the respect of the whole world for the statesmanlike – even saintly – way in which he accepted and wielded political power in the new South Africa. Thanks to his leadership, there were no revenge killings, there was no bloodbath. Against all expectations, the liberation of black South Africa proved to be a happy rite of passage. Known as the Father of the Nation, he is deeply revered within South Africa, where he is affectionately spoken of as *Madiba* (his Xhosa tribal name), or *Tata* (Father). Mandela's genius lies not merely in leadership but in self-control and benevolence. He is recognized worldwide as a great man of charisma, peace and justice who is the epitome of fundamental goodness, dignity and righteousness.

On 5 December 2013, Nelson Mandela died at the age of 95 after suffering from a prolonged respiratory infection. His death received worldwide media coverage and at least 80 foreign heads of state travelled to Qunu in the Eastern Cape, for the state funeral on 15 December, attended by over 4,500 people.

> *"There is nothing like returning to a place that remains unchanged to find the ways in which you yourself have altered."*

Nelson Mandela following his release
from Robben Island prison, 1990.

HENRI MATISSE

The Creative Courage of Innovation

BIOGRAPHY

NAME:	Henri-Émile-Benoît Matisse	**NATIONALITY:**	French
BORN:	December 31, 1869 Le Cateau-Cambrésis, Nord, France	**OCCUPATION:**	Painter, draughtsman, printmaker, sculptor
DIED:	November 3, 1954 (Aged 84) Nice, Alpes-Maritimes, France		

The French artist, Henri Matisse, was born in 1869 and grew up in Picardy, in northern France. In 1887, he went to Paris to study law and after qualifying, worked as a court official. While he was convalescing after an attack of appendicitis in 1889, his mother thoughtfully gave him paints and brushes to occupy him, and this episode at the age of 20 was his first attempt at painting. He found in it what he later described as 'a kind of paradise' and decided he wanted to pursue a career in art; his father, who ran a flower business, was deeply disappointed.

In 1891, Matisse went back to Paris to study art formally with William-Adolphe Bouguereau and Gustave Moreau, painting proficient landscapes and still-lifes in the style of Poussin, Watteau and Chardin, whose work he particularly admired. But he also imitated modern painters like Manet.

He was lucky to be taught by Gustave Moreau, a fine painter, but also an inspirational teacher who encouraged his students to develop their own individual artistic personalities and styles. He was an unusual teacher, who eagerly joined in his pupils' adventures in stylistic development.

In 1896, Matisse went to Brittany to visit John Peter Russell, who introduced him to the Impressionist style – and to the work of van Gogh, whose work was at that time completely unknown. But Russell had been a friend of van Gogh's, and showed Matisse some of his paintings. This visit was a rite of passage, completely changing the way Matisse painted. 'Russell was my teacher, and Russell explained colour theory to me.' That year, Matisse exhibited five paintings in the Beaux-Arts salon.

In 1898, Matisse travelled to London to see the paintings of Turner, on the advice of Camille Pissarro. He was immersing himself in the work of other painters, even buying contemporary work that he especially admired. He collected a bust by Rodin, a drawing by van Gogh and paintings by Gauguin and Cézanne, who was to become his main inspiration.

From 1904 to 1908 Matisse and others (including his remarkable teacher, Moreau) launched the Fauve style, which used wild, garish and unnatural colour – almost like jazz in paint. One of their exhibitions, in 1905, was severely lambasted by the critics, who said, 'A pot of paint has been flung in the face of the public.' But Matisse was not completely demoralized as one of his paintings was bought by the American writer, Gertrude Stein.

Matisse worked in Montparnasse, the famous artistic and intellectual district of Paris on the left bank of the Seine, alongside many other avant-garde artists and writers of the time. But he did not fit in well – he dressed conservatively and had strictly middle-class work habits. He was not at all the typical Parisian artist.

"I don't paint things. I only paint the difference between things."

He absorbed new influences, African and Islamic art, while visiting Morocco in 1912. This experience led him to use black as a colour and be bolder in his use of intense flat colours. He had met Pablo Picasso, who was 12 years younger, in 1906. The two became life-long friends and artistic rivals of contrasting styles. Matisse liked to work from nature, while Picasso preferred working from memory and imagination. At this time, Matisse's main collectors and supporters were Americans in Paris – Gertrude Stein and her two brothers Leo and Michael, and two friends from Baltimore, Claribel and Etta Cone.

The Cones became major patrons of Picasso and Matisse, and their collection can now be seen in the Baltimore Museum of Art. Picasso and Matisse became regular guests at Gertrude Stein's Saturday evening salons. She attributed these *soirées* to Matisse's initiative – 'Matisse brought people, everybody brought somebody, and they came at any time and it began to be a nuisance, and it was in this way that Saturday evenings began.'

In 1917, Matisse left Paris for the south of France, moving to a suburb of Nice. The softening and relaxation of his art over the next decade was characteristic of a great deal of post-war art; it has been described as 'a return to order'. But some critics found Matisse's quieter paintings shallow and decorative.

After 1930, perhaps symptomatic of the decade itself, Matisse's art became bolder, more vigorous. This was the period of *The Dance*, perhaps his best-known painting. Then there was a period of personal decline. He and his wife of 41 years separated in 1939. In 1941 he had a colostomy. After that he spent a lot of time in a wheelchair. But he went on working. Helped by assistants, he created paper collages, often on a large scale. He called this technique 'painting with scissors'.

Matisse died of a heart attack at the age of 84, in 1954. His 50-year-long career in art began by absorbing a very large number of influences. He responded to these and in his turn became a major influencer of other artists. His stylistic innovations fundamentally changed the course of modern art.

Picasso famously painted *Guernica*, and there is no equivalent in Matisse's output. But the art of Matisse remained undisturbed by the events of the 20th century, and in this way he is a refreshing foil to Picasso.

His reputation was impressive during his lifetime, but now, 60 years after his death, his standing is greater than ever, not least because of his huge impact on modern American abstract art after World War II. Matisse's principle that colour is the key to the configuration of a picture became essential to American abstract artists. So it was that, right at the end of his life, Matisse was confirmed as one of the great decisive figures in the pantheon of 20th century art.

"A picture must possess a real power to generate light and for a long time now I've been conscious of expressing myself through light or rather in light."

ROGER PENROSE

The Road to Reality

BIOGRAPHY ━━━━━━━━━━━━━━━━━━━━━━━━━━━━━━━━━━━━━━

NAME: Roger Penrose

BORN: August 8, 1931
Colchester, Essex, England,
United Kingdom

NATIONALITY: British

OCCUPATION: Mathematician, physicist,
philosopher

The mathematician and physicist Sir Roger Penrose was born in Colchester, Essex, England in 1931. His brother Oliver is a mathematician and another brother Jonathan is a chess grandmaster. Roger went to University College School, then University College, London, where he was awarded a first-class degree in mathematics. He went on to gain a PhD at Cambridge University in 1958; the subject was algebraic geometry. He devised the Penrose triangle, which he described as 'impossibility in its purest form'. He exchanged ideas with M. C. Escher, the artist, whose depictions of impossible objects had been a partial inspiration for the triangle. Penrose went on to design a staircase that simultaneously goes up and down. Escher was himself influenced by Penrose when he produced his *Waterfall* and *Ascending and Descending*.

In 1967, Roger Penrose devised his twistor theory. This maps geometric objects into four-dimensional space. Then, two years later, he put forward the cosmic censorship hypothesis: that the universe protects us from the inherent unpredictability of singularities, like the singularity in the middle of a black hole, by hiding them from us behind an event horizon, a boundary beyond which we cannot see. This is called the 'weak censorship hypothesis'. In 1979, Penrose proposed a 'strong censorship hypothesis'. It is said that settling the censorship conjectures is one of the most important outstanding problems in general relativity.

Roger Penrose also put forward the Weyl Curvature Hypothesis in 1979, which relates to the initial conditions of the observable part of the universe and the origin of the second law of thermodynamics. James Terrell and Roger Penrose realized, independently of one another, that objects travelling close to the speed of light must appear to skew or rotate. This effect has become known as Penrose-Terrell rotation.

Penrose's fertile mind also produced, or discovered, Penrose tilings. These are surfaces that are made of two kinds of geometric tiles that can only tile a plane non-periodically; they are also the first tilings to show five-fold rotational symmetry. He discovered or invented this tiling in 1974; then, in 1984, similar patterns were observed in nature, in atoms in quasi-crystals.

Roger Penrose became a popularizer of causal diagrams, now commonly known as Penrose diagrams. In 2004, he published *The Road to Reality: A Complete Guide to the Laws of the Universe*. This attempts to be a comprehensive guide to the laws of physics. It is, dauntingly, more than a thousand pages long.

In 2010, Penrose reported what may be evidence of an earlier universe that existed before the Big Bang that initiated our present universe. The so-called 'CMB Sky' is the sky as seen in a microwave map, and what that shows is the fairly uniform low-level radiation that is still there, left over from the Big Bang. What Penrose noticed was that, within the CMB Sky map, it is possible to detect the presence of concentric circles thought not to have been produced by the Big Bang.

"There are two other words I do not understand – awareness and intelligence."

Roger Penrose has been awarded several prizes, including the Wolf Prize, which he and Stephen Hawking shared in 1988, in recognition of their contribution to our understanding of the universe. He is the origin of a great many of the modern ideas about the universe that we (so quickly) have taken for granted. It was Roger Penrose who proposed, back in 1965, that singularities like black holes might be formed as a result of the gravitational collapse of huge, dying stars; now the idea that black holes are implosion features has become generally accepted.

Roger Penrose, now Sir Roger Penrose, OM, is celebrated for his work in physics and cosmology. Many of his ideas have broken boundaries, and some have been challenged. One of his ideas (from the 1989 book *The Emperor's New Mind*) has proved particularly controversial: that consciousness could not be explained by existing scientific principles. Penrose uses a complex argument based on the interaction of 'on-off' machines.

Because, ultimately the on-or-off state of any one of the machines is determined by the on-or-off state of another machine, the end result is ultimately predetermined. From there, Penrose argues that the present generation of computers can never display intelligence, because they are run on the on-off principle. The human mind is clearly not dominated by this kind of interacting on-off sub-system and could never be matched by even a very complex computer made up of huge numbers of on-off sub-systems.

Penrose of course has opponents, and among those are mathematicians and philosophers, and computer scientists who support the idea of artificial intelligence, but Penrose maintains that the way human beings think transcends formal logic. Perhaps he hopes to discover a new basic principle of physics that will account for consciousness – that would be the greatest breakthrough of all.

No-one seriously expects a scientist functioning at this dizzying level to be right about everything. What is remarkable about Roger Penrose is the steady flow of brilliant new ideas, new theories about the cosmos, coming from his mind – however it works.

Roger Penrose has no religious faith and describes himself as an atheist and a humanist. 'I think I would say that the universe has a purpose. It's not somehow just there by chance … Some people, I think, take the view that the universe is just there and it runs along – it's a bit like it just sort of computes, and we happen somehow by accident to find ourselves in this thing. But I don't think that's a very fruitful or helpful way of looking at the universe. I think there is something much deeper about it.'

"Intelligence cannot be present without understanding. No computer has any awareness of what it does."

PABLO PICASSO

Everything You Can Imagine is Real

Pablo Picasso was born in Málaga in Andalusia in 1881. His father was an artist and professor at the Academy of Fine Arts in Barcelona. The young Pablo naturally had his first lessons in art from his father. When he was 14, he entered the academy at Barcelona. Two years later he transferred to Madrid for advanced training, and quickly became a master of the traditional techniques of painting. Picasso's early work shows him as a talented illustrator, though in a rather sentimental style, and this sentimentality can still be seen later in his blue period paintings.

In 1898 Picasso won a gold medal for his painting *Customs of Aragon*, which was exhibited in his home town. Three years later, he set himself up in a Paris studio in Montmartre and though he was a Catalan by birth he made France his home for the rest of his life. Paris was the natural haven for artists at that time.

Picasso quickly absorbed the Neo-Impressionist influences of the Paris school, as seen in the work of Toulouse-Lautrec, Degas and Vuillard, painting works such as *The Blue Room* (1904). In his blue period, 1902–4, he painted a series of haunting but depressing interiors. In the pink period that followed, 1904–6, he produced a contrasting series of harlequins and acrobats. Toulouse-Lautrec had painted the bars and the music halls, Degas had painted the ballet, now Picasso painted the circus.

He never stayed long in the same waters, and he moved quickly forward to explore what African art could teach him. He was fascinated by the simplified, reductive forms of African sculpture in particular. This preoccupation produced the transitional *Two Nudes* (1906), which heralded a major break with traditional styles, and a breakthrough into a series of distinctively new '20th century' styles. The landmark work was *Les Demoiselles d'Avignon* of 1906, the first full-blown Cubist painting.

The principle of Cubism was to render three-dimensional objects on canvas without resorting to perspective. Instead of describing objects, the new style allowed the artist to analyze them and present what he regarded as their key features; facets as seen from several different vantage points might be re-assembled in the painting to create an entirely new and perhaps unrecognizable form. It was in its way more like music than the 19th century concept of visual art, though it was still not quite fully abstract.

It was certainly a more thoughtful and thought-provoking approach to visual art than people were used to seeing. Many people hated it and ridiculed Picasso for being incapable of drawing 'properly'. This perception, and the rift that it created between serious artists and the general public, was to prove a problem for many decades. Ordinary people were still ridiculing the avant-garde Picasso and his 'modern art' long after his death.

"Art is a lie that makes us realize truth."

Georges Braque was at the same time experimenting with strong colours, with a group including Matisse calling themselves Les Fauves, but from 1909 until 1914 he joined forces with Picasso in exploring the possibilities of Cubism. Picasso and Braque experimented with collage and mixed media techniques, including incorporating bits of wood and wire in the composition.

In 1917, Picasso became associated with Diaghilev's Russian Ballet, designing costumes and sets for *Parade*, *Pulcinella* and *Le Train Bleu*. For these, he used both Cubist and Neo-Classical styles, which was a clever way of making Cubism more accessible to the public. *Three Dancers* (1925) contains grotesque distortions of the

Guernica by Pablo Picasso, 1937.

human body, following Cubist principles, and prepared the way for the grotesqueness of what has become Picasso's most famous piece of work, *Guernica* (1937).

Guernica is a huge canvas, on which Picasso expressed his horror at the bombing of a Basque town during the Spanish Civil War, and his abomination of war in general. It has become a classic art work, with the same status as Leonardo's *Mona Lisa*, Michelangelo's *David* or Constable's *Hay Wain*: it is recognized as great art. Picasso became director of the Prado Gallery in Madrid in 1936, but during World War II, in spite of being stoutly anti-Nazi, he spent most of his time in occupied Paris. He took a risk in staying there during the German occupation; he just carried on as usual, like Archimedes during the Greek invasion of Syracuse.

After the war, he became a Communist, but neither the visual nightmare *Guernica* nor his portrait of Stalin painted in 1953 endeared him to the Communist Party. His was not the art of the people, by a long way. Yet the 1949 Paris Communist World Peace Conference was ready to use the dove of peace that he painted as its logo.

Picasso designed more stage sets, illustrated translations of classical texts, tried his hand at sculpture and in later life simply-painted ceramics. He was one of the most fluent, versatile and eclectic painters who ever lived. He was also extremely accessible and uninhibited. Unlike most artists, he was ready to let film-makers come into his studio and film him at work. He made it difficult for Picasso-enthusiasts to keep up with him, as he was always innovating. In a very real sense, his artistic career reflected the turmoil and swiftness of change that characterized every aspect of life in the 20th century.

Everything Picasso did was widely imitated and copied by his thousands of followers and admirers, assimilated into other arts and every aspect of design, including the architecture of Frank Lloyd Wright and Le Corbusier. It is easy to see the influence of Picasso's Cubist paintings in the mid-20th century sculptures of Henry Moore and Barbara Hepworth. Picasso was the paramount influence on 20th century art.

"Painting is a blind man's profession. He paints not what he sees, but what he feels, what he tells himself about what he has seen."

MAX PLANCK

The Great Unfathomable Question

BIOGRAPHY ━━━

NAME: Max Karl Ernst Ludwig Planck

BORN: April 23, 1858
Kiel, Duchy of Holstein,
Germany

DIED: October 4, 1947 (Aged 89)
Göttingen, Lower Saxony,
Germany

NATIONALITY: German

OCCUPATION: Theoretical physicist

MAX PLANCK

Max Planck, the German scientist who created a revolution in 20th century physics, was born into a traditional and intellectual family in Kiel, in 1858. His father was a professor of law; his uncle was a judge and his grandfather and great-grandfather were professors of theology at Göttingen University. Curiously, he was baptized with the name 'Marx', perhaps intended as a contraction of 'Markus', but he always signed himself 'Max'. In 1867, the Planck family moved to Munich, where young Max enrolled at the gymnasium (an academic secondary school, equivalent to English grammar school or American prep school). The mathematics teacher there, Hermann Müller, found the boy interesting, and taught him astronomy and mechanics as well as maths. Müller taught Planck the principle of conservation of energy and gave him his first sight of physics.

Max Planck was not only a mathematician: he had a gift for music too. He sang and played the piano, organ and cello; he composed songs; he composed operas. But in the end physics was his chosen subject. The physics professor at Munich, Philipp von Jolly, advised Planck *not* to go in for physics as it was a field where 'almost everything is already discovered, and all that remains is to fill a few holes'. Planck's careful and revealing answer was that *he did not want to discover new things*, only to understand the subject.

Studying under von Jolly from 1874, Planck undertook the only scientific experiments he was ever to perform. His field from there on was to be theoretical physics. In 1877, Planck went to Berlin to study with the physicists von Helmholtz and Kirchhoff, but both were disappointing to him, and he fell back on self-education. He graduated in 1878, presenting two dissertations in 1879 and 1880. The second of these, his habilitation thesis, enabled him to teach. To begin with, no-one was interested in giving him a lectureship, but eventually in 1885 he became associate professor of theoretical physics at Kiel University.

After working on entropy, Planck became professor at Berlin University. In 1907, he was offered a similar post in Vienna, but declined in order to remain in Berlin, where he stayed until he retired in 1926. Several other professors at Berlin University lived close to Planck's house, which soon became a social and cultural hub, with music forming an important element in the gatherings. Many scientists, Einstein among them, were frequent visitors.

During World War I, Planck's eldest son Karl was killed at Verdun; his second son Erwin had already been taken prisoner by the French. His two daughters both died in childbirth shortly after the war. Planck suffered these losses with stoicism. Right at the end of World War II came the final blow, when Erwin was executed by the Gestapo for his participation in the plot to assassinate Hitler. Planck and his son were very close, and the old man lost the will to live; he died not long after this traumatic event.

Planck's lectures were dry and impersonal, but he spoke without notes and never made a mistake; one student described him as 'the best lecturer I ever heard'. Like the rest of his family, he was naturally conservative and cautious, and disliked revolutionary ideas; he did not really want to find out something that would overturn classical physics. But he trusted logic absolutely, and it was this that led him into a revolution in physics. As Max Born wrote, 'He did not hesitate to express a claim contradicting all tradition, because he had convinced himself that no other resort was possible.'

"No burden is so heavy for a man to bear as a succession of happy days."

In 1900 he put forward his devastatingly new idea, the Planck Postulate, that electromagnetic energy can only be emitted in a quantized form, as a multiple of a basic unit $E = hv$, where E is energy, h is Planck's constant and v is the frequency of the radiation. Physicists now call these 'quanta' photons; the amplitude of energy at a particular frequency is a function of the number of photons of that frequency being produced.

At first, Planck did not realize what he had done, he 'did not think much about it', but it later became clear that this was a breakthrough, the birth of quantum physics. It was in effect the biggest achievement of Planck's career. Discovering the constant enabled Planck to define a new set of physical units, such as the Planck mass and the Planck length, all based on physical constants.

Einstein realized some of the implications of Planck's idea in 1905, and it has been commented that Einstein ought to be given more credit for quantum physics than Planck, because Planck did not see that he was introducing the quantum as a real physical entity. Whatever the truth, Planck was awarded the Nobel Prize in Physics in 1918.

In 1905, the still-unknown Einstein's three major papers were published. Planck was one of the few who understood the far-reaching significance of Einstein's Theory of Relativity, and it was Planck who saw to it that others recognized it too. Planck became Dean of Berlin University and in that position he was in 1914 able to establish a new chair and invite Einstein to occupy it. Once Einstein was in Berlin, the two men were able to meet more, play music more, and develop their ideas.

Later Planck tried to grasp the meaning of energy quanta, but he was unable to find it. His attempts 'extended over several years and caused me much trouble'. But other physicists were having difficulties with Planck's constant too.

In the years following World War II, Planck was regarded as the leading German physicist, but the worsening economic situation in Germany made it very difficult for any research to continue. Elsewhere, scientists worked on a theory of quantum mechanics, but Planck rejected it, believing that in the near future developments in wave mechanics would render quantum theory redundant. He was hoping to be wrong. He was still a very reluctant revolutionary.

But continuing work only seemed to add support to quantum theory, even though he and Einstein regretted it. He came to a sad conclusion; 'A new scientific truth does not triumph by convincing its opponents and making them see sense, but rather because its opponents eventually die, and a new generation grows up that is familiar with it.' Planck was a very rare individual; he had an astonishingly original idea – and wished that he hadn't.

"Whence come I and whither go I? That is the great unfathomable question, the same for everyone of us. Science has no answer to it."

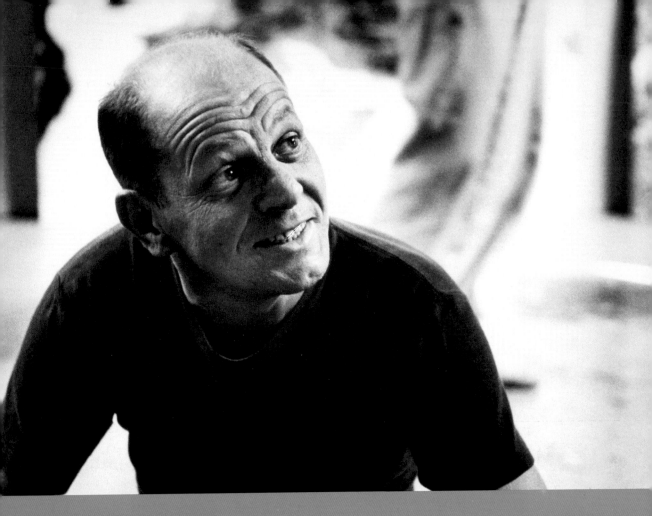

JACKSON POLLOCK

Every Painting has a Life of its Own

BIOGRAPHY ━━━━━━

NAME: Paul Jackson Pollock

BORN: January 28, 1912
Cody, Wyoming, United States

DIED: August 11, 1956 (Aged 44)
Springs, New York,
United States

NATIONALITY: American

OCCUPATION: Painter

Jackson Pollock was born in Wyoming, USA in 1912 of Presbyterian parents. His father was a farmer and later a land surveyor. The young Jackson Pollock grew up in the states of Arizona and California, where he was twice expelled from school. While still a boy, he accompanied his father on surveying trips, and during these he had some significant encounters with Native American culture, including sand-artists.

In 1930 he followed his brother Charles to New York; they both studied art under Thomas Hart Benton at the Art Students League. Benton's work had traditional rural American culture as its subject matter, and Pollock's work was influenced by this only fleetingly. But Benton's rhythmic use of paint and his determined independence of mind were to be strong and lasting influences on him.

Jackson Pollock's big problem was drink. He was an alcoholic, and from 1938 to 1941 he underwent Jungian analysis with Joseph Henderson, hoping for a cure. Dr Henderson engaged Pollock through his art and encouraged him to make drawings to explore his unconscious. This led to the appearance of Jungian concepts in Pollock's paintings. It is thought now that Pollock may have suffered from bipolar disorder.

In 1945, Pollock married another painter, Lee Krasner, who became an important influence on his work, and they moved to Springs on Long Island. Peggy Guggenheim lent them the deposit so that they could buy a timber-frame house with a barn, and Pollock converted the barn into a studio. There he refined the new technique of painting which he pioneered and with which he will always be associated. He came across liquid paints at an experimental workshop in 1936, and in the early 1940s he used his technique of pouring liquid paint to create several canvases. After the move to Springs, he started producing canvases horizontally, laying them out flat on the studio floor. Because he could walk all round and across the canvas, the paint could be applied from all directions; this was very different from the creation of a painting on an easel. He then developed a combination of pouring and dripping techniques. He started using the new generation of household paints instead of conventional artists' paints. It was, as he said, 'a natural growth out of a need'. To apply the paint, he used a variety of tools, including hardened brushes, sticks and basting syringes.

> *"I want to express my feelings rather than illustrate them."*

The intensely physical process of painting that Pollock was developing made the splashes and streaks of paint into direct expressions of the movements of his entire body as he created the canvas. The image that resulted in effect recorded the action by which it had been created, a kind of frozen dance. The new style became known as 'action painting'. Pollock explained his concept and technique in an interview:

> 'My painting does not come from the easel. I prefer to tack the unstretched canvas to the hard wall or the floor. I need the resistance of a hard surface. On the floor I am more at ease. I feel nearer, more part of the painting, since this way I can walk around it, work from the four sides and literally be in the painting ...
>
> 'When I am in my painting, I'm not aware of what I'm doing. It is only after a sort of get-acquainted period that I see what I have been about. I have no fear of making changes, destroying the image, etc, because the painting has a life of its own. I try to let it come through. It is only when I lose contact with the painting that the result is a mess. Otherwise there is pure harmony, an easy give and take, and the painting comes out well.'

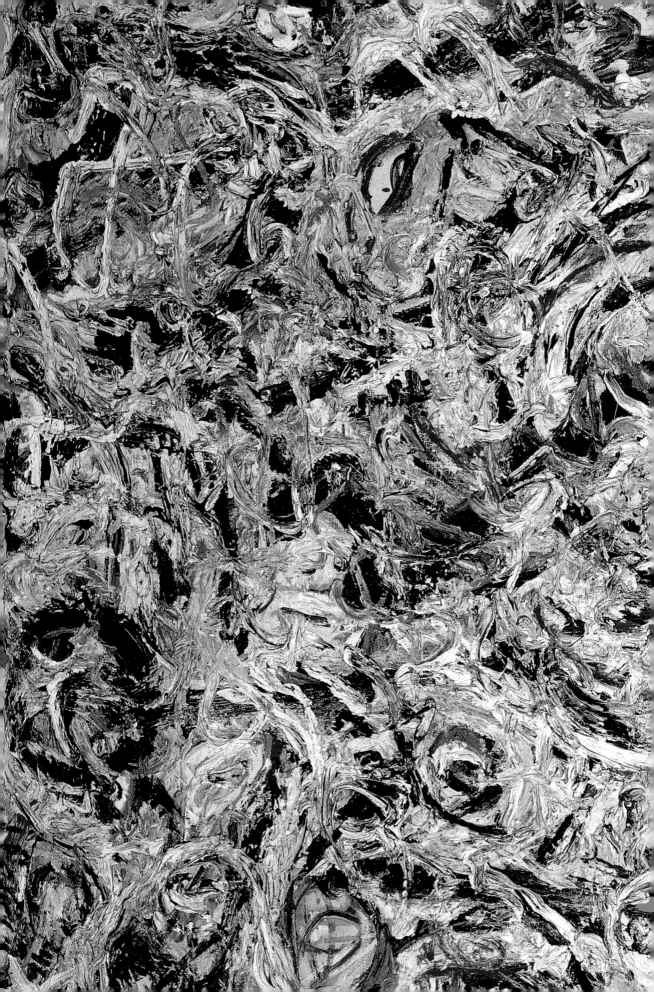

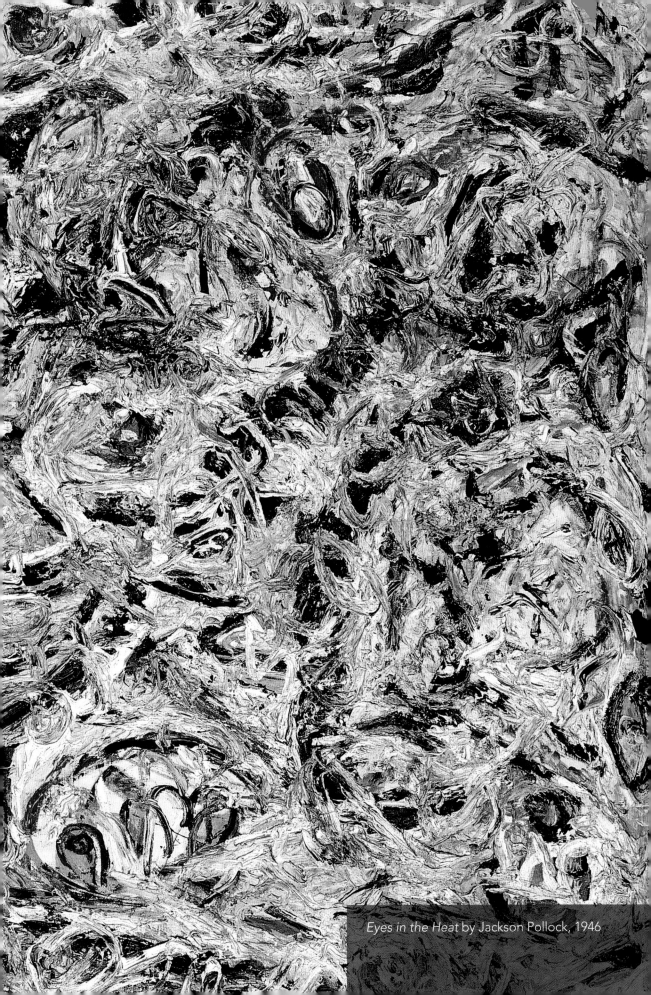

Eyes in the Heat by Jackson Pollock, 1946

But he was clear that the paintings were not accidental. He had a view of how he wanted a painting to look. He used the movement of his body, over which he had control, the viscous flow of paint, the force of gravity, and the absorption of paint into the canvas. He was exploiting a calculated combination of controllable and uncontrollable factors. He moved energetically round the canvas, almost as if he was dancing, throwing, dripping, pouring and spattering, and did not stop until he saw the image that he wanted. The process was, in his own words, 'akin to the methods of the [Native American] sand-painters of the West'.

Like many a pioneer in the arts, Pollock was greeted with about equal measures of admiration and scorn. Many derided him and what seemed to be the most extreme form that modern art could take. In 1956, *Time* magazine called him Jack the Dripper. Admirers read perhaps too much into his art. Some claimed that he incorporated mathematical fractals, that he was representing mathematical chaos a decade before Chaos Theory was invented. Detractors have claimed that Pollock was happy to allow popular theories to become attached to his work in order to create an illusion of depth of meaning – meaning that isn't really there.

A major innovation in Jackson Pollock's paintings is the 'all-over' effect. There are no blank areas or highlight areas, there is no positive area, no negative area. The lines in his paintings do not describe the edges of anything; the lines cannot be made to represent objects in the real world, even by a process of projection. The paintings do not therefore represent anything and are purely abstract. The gesture recorded on the canvas is a gesture of liberation from values of any kind, whether political, aesthetic or moral. Some have seen this as a backward step in art, and denounced Pollock's drip paintings as little more than animal. But, if so, it is hard to see how the paint texture comes across as so consistently and masterfully controlled; the paint surface is almost balletic.

Jackson Pollock's drip period did not last long, only from 1947 to 1950, but this was the Jackson Pollock who became famous. *Life* magazine asked in 1949, 'Is he the greatest living painter in the United States?' But he moved on to painting in black on unprimed canvas, then back to colour, then added representational elements. He was now working with a more commercial gallery and trying to cope with the demand for his work. He became frustrated and his alcoholism worsened.

He died in a drink-driving accident, his own car the only vehicle involved, with Pollock himself at the wheel, in August 1956. At the age of 44, his career was over. It was a career of innovation, achievement and intense frustration. Pollock will be remembered for the drip paintings created between 1947 and 1950, and they are highly sought after by collectors. In 2006, *No. 5, 1948* was bought for $140 million.

"Abstract painting is abstract. It confronts you."

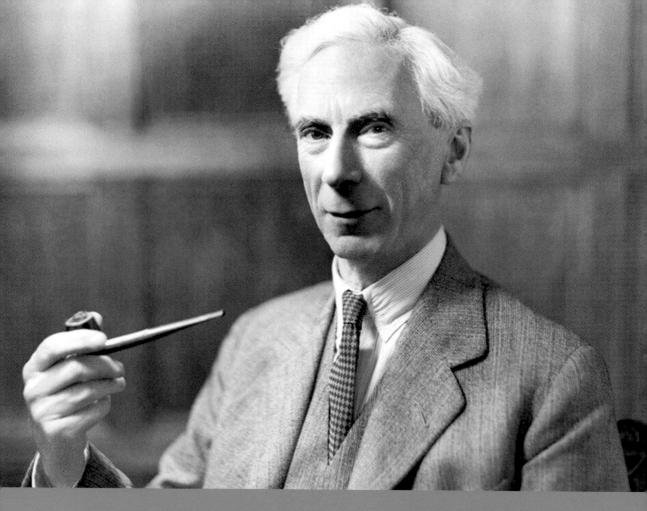

BERTRAND RUSSELL

Western Philosophy and the Everyday World

BIOGRAPHY

NAME: Bertrand Arthur William Russell

BORN: May 18, 1872
Trellech, Gwent, Wales,
United Kingdom

DIED: February 2, 1970 (Aged 97)
Penrhyndeudraeth, Wales,
United Kingdom

NATIONALITY: British

OCCUPATION: Philosopher, logician,
mathematician, historian,
pacifist

Bertrand Russell, 3rd Earl Russell, was born at Trellech in Gwent, Wales in 1872. His parents died when he was only three and he was brought up by his grandmother, the widow of the Liberal Prime Minister, Lord John Russell. To add to the unusualness of his upbringing, he was educated by governesses and tutors before going to Trinity College, Cambridge. This was for him a difficult rite of passage, as he had to adjust suddenly and at a very late stage to education in company, and initially he was hampered by shyness. He gained a degree in mathematics and philosophy in 1894.

For a short time, Russell was a British Embassy official in Paris, but became a fellow of Trinity College in 1895, shortly after marrying Alys Smith. He visited Berlin and on the strength of that visit wrote his first book, *German Social Democracy*. This marked the beginning of a long and wide-ranging intellectual career. After his return to England from Germany, Bertrand and Alys lived at Haslemere, Surrey, where he devoted himself to philosophy.

Russell's most original contributions to mathematics, logic and philosophy were made in the period before 1914. His outstanding works in the field of mathematics were *The Principles of Mathematics*, in which he argued that all mathematics could be derived from logic, and *Principia Mathematica*, where he developed the idea fully. *Principia* stands as a landmark in the development of both disciplines.

The young Wittgenstein came to Cambridge to be Russell's student in 1912–13. Ten years later, Russell was to write the introduction to Wittgenstein's *Tractatus*.

Russell was a great academic: but he was also a great popularizer of his subject. His first populist book was *The Problems of Philosophy*, which came out in 1912. World War I broke across his intellectual career in 1914 and he became immersed in political issues. He was a militant pacifist, which caused Trinity College to strip him of his Fellowship in 1916 and the authorities to imprison him in 1918. Russell was forced to make his living by lecturing and journalism, and he went out of his way to become a well-known controversialist; now he needed to be noticed. He knew and argued with D. H. Lawrence.

He briefly visited the Soviet Union immediately after the Revolution, and met Lenin. Russell asked Lenin how people with different views would be accommodated in the new system and was startled by Lenin's instant savage reply: 'We will shoot them!' Of course, Russell should have known that that would be the case, but he was still struck by Lenin's gangsterish barbarism. He also met Trotsky and Gorky.

The Russian experience sobered Russell considerably; from that point on he was less enthusiastic about communism. He wrote *Practice and Theory of Bolshevism*. Even more remarkably, in the same year Russell visited China, where he lectured on philosophy at Beijing University. By now he was divorced from Alys, and in 1921 he married Dora Black. The need to earn money was everpresent and he wrote more popular works, such as *The ABC of Atoms* and *The ABC of Relativity*.

"War does not determine who is right - only who is left."

Bertrand Russell went on being controversial between the two World Wars. His impending second divorce (1935) led him to reflect on *Marriage and Morals* in 1929. In 1942 his lectureship at City College, New York was terminated on the grounds that he was 'an enemy of religion and morality'. He did however eventually win damages for wrongful dismissal. The rise of fascism in Europe led him to renounce his pacifism in 1939. His Fellowship at Trinity College, Cambridge was accordingly restored in 1944. He returned to England after the war ended, and was awarded the Order of Merit. He also produced the best-selling book *History of Western Philosophy*, which offers a panoramic, detailed, beautifully written and wholly accessible view of a very difficult subject – a truly remarkable book.

His journalistic side drove him to publish a stream of provocative pieces, such as *Why I am not a Christian* (1957). The Cold War and the development of huge stores of nuclear weapons alarmed him greatly, and he took a leading role in the British Campaign for Nuclear Disarmament (CND). In connection with this cause, Russell, who was now an international celebrity, launched into correspondence with all the major political leaders of the world, as well as participating in CND rallies. In 1961, he found himself in prison, again, for his part in a sit-down demonstration in London outside the British Parliament buildings in Whitehall.

To the end – and he lived to be almost 100 – he retained his resolute independence of mind, his lucidity of argument and his chirpy sense of humour. Russell's importance as a philosopher lies in his role as a clear and logical commentator on a wide range of 20th century intellectual and moral issues, and on his application of logical analysis to ethical and metaphysical matters. He showed that it is possible to construct a morality without falling back on a religious faith. His academic work in mathematics and philosophy carried both disciplines forward, and his popular works brought many new ideas to ordinary people.

When the German philosopher Martin Heidegger tried to engage with the larger world outside the lecture room, he failed abysmally, but when Bertrand Russell reached out to it he was hugely successful. Given Russell's closeted and aristocratic upbringing, this success in the everyday world is all the more surprising. It is certainly not what might have been foretold when little Bertrand was orphaned at the age of three.

"To understand the actual world as it is, not as we should wish it to be, is the beginning of wisdom."

JEAN-PAUL SARTRE

The Illusion of Being Eternal

"There is only one day left, always starting over; it is given to us at dawn and taken away from us at dusk."

BIOGRAPHY

NAME: Jean-Paul Charles Aymard Sartre

BORN: June 21, 1905
Paris, France

DIED: April 15, 1980 (Aged 74)
Paris, France

NATIONALITY: French

OCCUPATION: Existentialist philosopher, playwright, novelist, screenwriter, political activist, biographer, literary critic

Sartre's father Jean-Baptiste was a naval officer and his mother Anne-Marie was the cousin of the medical missionary Albert Schweitzer. His father died while Jean-Paul was still a baby, and Anne-Marie moved back into her parents' house in Meudon, in the south-west suburbs of Paris. It was Jean-Paul's grandfather who taught him mathematics and introduced him to classical literature. When he was 12, his mother remarried and they moved to La Rochelle, on France's west coast, where he was the victim of bullying.

From 1924 to 1929, Sartre was a student at a college of higher education in Paris. With other students, he organized a hoax following Charles Lindbergh's flight across the Atlantic. They persuaded the press that Lindbergh was to be awarded an honorary degree. The event was duly announced in the press. Huge numbers of people turned up at the college, where Sartre and his friends laid on a Lindbergh look-alike. There was a public outcry when the hoax was exposed and the college director Gustave Lanson resigned. Sartre commented in 1939 that 'There is more destructive power [in pranks] than in all the works of Lenin.'

Between pranks, Sartre worked hard, and gained his PhD. He then travelled to Berlin to study the philosophies of Edmund Husserl and Martin Heidegger and took several successive teaching posts.

Sartre was conscripted into the French Army from 1929 to 1931. Thirty years later he argued that every French person was responsible for the crimes committed during the Algerian War of Independence. In 1939, he found himself called up again, this time as a meteorologist. He was captured by the Germans in 1940 and spent nine months as a prisoner-of-war.

While a prisoner he read Heidegger's *Being and Time*, which became a major influence. His health deteriorated (he claimed his poor eyesight affected his balance) and the Germans released him. He took a teaching position vacated by a Jewish teacher who had been banned from teaching by the Vichy government – a significant ethical dilemma for a moral philosopher.

Returning to Paris in 1941, with a group of other writers and students he co-founded an underground group called Socialism and Liberty. He tried to enlist André Malraux and André Gide, but they were reluctant to join and Sartre seems to have lost confidence. He decided to write instead of involving himself in active resistance to the Germans. Out of this came *Being and Nothingness* and *No Exit*, which went uncensored by the Germans.

But there was a price to pay for his actions during the German occupation. Sartre was a high-profile contributor to the newspaper *Combat*, which was founded during the occupation by Albert Camus, a philosopher and writer with similar views to Sartre. During this immediate post-war period, when Sartre was extremely popular, many liked to see him as a Resistance activist, if not an actual fighter. But the genuinely 'Resistant' Vladimir Jankelevitch drew attention to Sartre's lack of political commitment during the German occupation and presented his 'struggles for liberty' as an attempt to redeem himself. Camus himself, though a friend of Sartre, described him as a writer who resisted, not a resister who wrote; in other words, with Sartre the writing had always come first.

> *"Life has no meaning the moment you lose the illusion of being eternal."*

Sartre remained politically active in the post-war period, in 1960 travelling to Cuba to meet Fidel Castro and Che Guevara, whom he saw as 'the most complete human being of our age … he lived his words, spoke his own actions, and his story and the story of the world ran parallel.' One senses in this a wistful backward glance at his own shortcomings in the 1940s in the face of the German occupation. Che Guevara had the courage to act, to fight, to give more than words, while he had not.

Sartre is one of those writers for whom a well-defined philosophical position lies at the centre of their being. He formulated and popularized a brand of existentialism that was drawn from many sources. One of those was Husserl's idea of a free, fully intentional consciousness; another was Heidegger's existentialism. He was also influenced by Kant, Hegel and Kierkegaard. But Sartre's existentialism remained a profoundly original creation. His personal popularity reached its peak in the 1940s, when his existentialist philosophy was also at its most popular.

Sartre and his life-long partner, Simone de Beauvoir, challenged the social and cultural assumptions embedded in their upbringing, which they rejected as bourgeois. They saw an inherent conflict between an authentic way of being and the oppressiveness and spiritual destructiveness of bourgeois conformism, a major theme of Sartre's early work and continued in *Being and Nothingness*.

Sartre's theoretical writings, his novels and his plays together form a major inspirational source in modern literature. An assumption throughout is that God does not exist. Man is condemned to freedom, a freedom from all authority, which he may seek to evade, distort or deny, but he has to face it if he is to become a moral being. The meaning of a human being's life is not fixed before his existence. Once the responsibility for freedom is acknowledged, man has to make this meaning for himself. The attempt to make oneself is futile without the support and solidarity of others.

Sartre reflected on the implications of this in his book *What is Literature?* (1948). Literature is not an activity for itself, but is concerned with human freedom and the author's commitment. Literature is committed. Artistic creation is a moral act.

His early psychological studies went more or less unnoticed by the general public. But his first novel, *Nausea* (1938), and a collection of short stories, *The Wall* (also 1938), brought him instant acclaim and success. Sartre's main work on philosophy, *Being and Nothingness* (1943), is a huge and structured exposition of his idea of being; from this book much of modern existentialism has flowed. He presented his ideas of existentialist humanism in a popular essay *Existentialism is a Humanism* (1946), and also developed them more accessibly in a series of novels called *The Roads to Freedom* (1945 – 49), based on his wartime experiences.

Sartre is also known as a playwright and as a literary critic. He was offered the 1964 Nobel Prize in Literature, but declined it, saying that he always declined official honours: 'a writer should not allow himself to be turned into an institution.' He had previously declined the *Lègion d'Honneur* in 1945.

He remained a fundamentally simple man, with few possessions, and he went on being politically engaged to the end. During the May 1968 strikes in Paris he was arrested for civil disobedience. President de Gaulle intervened to have him released, saying, 'You don't arrest Voltaire.'

Jean-Paul Sartre was above all one of the leading figures in 20th century French philosophy, whose work continues to influence Marxist philosophy, sociology, critical theory and literary studies.

"I'm going to smile, and my smile will sink down into your pupils, and heaven knows what it will become."

ARNOLD SCHOENBERG

Rewriting the Language of Music

QUOTE

"If it is art, it is not for all, and if it is for all, it is not art."

BIOGRAPHY

NAME: Arnold Schoenberg

BORN: September 13, 1874
Leopoldstadt, Vienna, Austria

DIED: July 13, 1951 (Aged 76)
Los Angeles, California,
United States

NATIONALITY: Austrian-American

OCCUPATION: Composer, arranger,
painter

The avant-garde Austrian composer Arnold Schoenberg was born into a lower-middle-class family (Lutheran, though of Jewish origin), in Vienna in 1874. His father was a shopkeeper and his mother was a piano teacher. Although there was some music in the family, Arnold was largely self-taught. Later he took lessons in counterpoint with the composer Zemlinsky, who became his brother-in-law. Schoenberg formally reverted to Judaism when Hitler came to power in 1933, then left Europe for America, where he taught in California and made friends with George Gershwin.

In his twenties, Schoenberg made a living orchestrating operas for other composers, while at the same time writing his own music. From 1901 to 1903, he was conducting a cabaret orchestra in Berlin. This was not a promising beginning, not the sort of beginning that one would expect for a career in music that would, with incredible ambition, seek to create an entirely new musical language. Nor is it easy, at that point in time, to see how Schoenberg could have become one of the most influential composers of the first half of the 20th century.

At first he wrote music that was strongly influenced by Wagner, such as the sextet *Verklärte Nacht* (*Transfigured Night*), which he later turned into an orchestral piece, and one of his most popular works. He also wrote the symphonic poem *Pelleas und Melisande* and the large-scale choral and orchestral piece *Gurrelieder*. It was appropriate that he should have been writing about transfiguration in the final months of the 19th century; he himself was about to transfigure Western music in the 20th century. Established composers of the stature of Richard Strauss and Gustav Mahler admired Schoenberg's early music, and saw him as a significant composer.

As his composing style changed he was able to influence others. Throughout his career he was a teacher, and his two most famous pupils, Webern and Berg, joined him in Vienna in 1904. A reaction to the German late Romantic style of Wagner was setting in. His *Second String Quartet* caused an uproar at its first performance in 1908. *Pierrot Lunaire* (1912) used an extremely chromatic

harmony that had its roots in, and therefore was a step back towards, Wagner's *Tristan und Isolde*.

By then, Strauss and Mahler were having difficulties. Strauss gave up on Schoenberg altogether. In a letter dated 1914, Schoenberg responded to an invitation; 'Dear Sir, I regret that I am unable to accept your invitation to write something for Richard Strauss's fiftieth birthday. In a letter to Frau Mahler, Herr Strauss wrote about me as follows: "The only person who can help poor Schoenberg now is a psychiatrist … I think he'd do better to shovel snow instead of scribbling on music-paper." '

Mahler, on the other hand, saw Schoenberg as his protégé and went on supporting him, even though he did not understand what his music was about. Schoenberg began by despising Mahler's music but when he heard Mahler's *Third Symphony* he was converted by 'the thunderbolt': he thought it was a work of genius. Schoenberg always spoke about Mahler in awed tones.

"I see the work as a whole first. Then I compose the details."

Schoenberg was in a major artistic crisis which, like the psychological crisis of Carl Jung, coincided with the four years of World War I. In the midst of this crisis, Schoenberg looked to the visual arts for a key to an escape route, and his own paintings were exhibited along with those of Kandinsky's group. The revolution that Picasso's Cubism created was something he himself was to mirror in music, a kind of fragmentation and re-assembly of the language of music.

In 1910, Schoenberg wrote his *Theory of Harmony*, which is one of the most influential books of the 20th century on music theory. By 1920, he had formulated his new musical language. It was constructed by a 12-note method, producing what is sometimes called serial music, in which a melodic line is built out of the 12 semitones of a scale, each note used once and only once. Because the new music rejected keys it was called 'atonal' (non-tonal).

This extraordinarily rigid and doctrinaire method of composing was so arid and restricting that Schoenberg himself gave it up eventually, returning to music based on keys. But, in the meantime, his pupils and other composers had taken it up and created a new fashion in music that ran parallel to abstract art in painting and sculpture – an art of the 20th century.

Arnold Schoenberg lived on until 1951, by which time he could see the destructive effects of his revolution in music. He influenced many significant composers: Alban Berg, Anton Webern, Egon Wellesz, and later John Cage. He left a legacy of two generations of classical music in the West that very few people wanted to listen to.

Young composers in the 1960s still felt honour-bound to compose in Schoenberg's 12-note style, and they mocked those who composed with tonal melody. Schoenberg was responsible for creating a virtually unbridgeable gap between serious composers and the general public. As a result of serial music, many people stopped bothering with serious music written in the 20th century altogether, switching to popular music instead.

Schoenberg was superstitious about numbers, which is where his 12-note idea arose. Twelve notes = good, but thirteen = bad. Schoenberg was very frightened of the number 13. He originally named his opera *Moses und Aaron*, but when he realized the title contained 13 letters he changed it to *Moses und Aron*: 12 letters. It appears he even frightened himself to death when someone pointed out that his age, 76, contained digits that added up to 13.

Schoenberg's idea for a new music was daring, brilliant and original, a genuine revolution in the way music might be constructed. The problem was that very few people wanted to listen to it and composers found extreme difficulties to compose creatively within its arbitrary rules.

Schoenberg was a visionary, but it was a misleading vision, one that has left a legacy of problems. His grave in Vienna is marked by a slightly misshapen cube of marble standing disconcertingly on one corner, an image that seems exactly right for an uneasy genius.

"My work should be judged as it enters the ears and heads of listeners, not as it is described to the eyes of readers."

IGOR STRAVINSKY

Composing the Music of Time

BIOGRAPHY ━━━

NAME: Igor Fyodorovich Stravinsky

BORN: June 17, 1882
Oranienbaum, near St
Petersburg, Russian Empire

DIED: April 6, 1971 (Aged 88)
Manhattan, New York,
United States

NATIONALITY: Russian / Naturalized
American

OCCUPATION: Composer, pianist,
conductor

The composer Igor Stravinsky was born in Oranienbaum (later renamed Lomonosov) in Russia. It was a troubled childhood; he felt that nobody had any real affection for him. His father, Fyodor Stravinsky, was a bass singer at the Mariinsky Theatre in St Petersburg, and young Igor took piano lessons and tried his hand at composition. Then in 1890 he saw Tchaikovsky's ballet *The Sleeping Beauty* at the Mariinsky Theatre. He was spellbound by the experience; it was the first time he had seen or heard an orchestra.

He was fired by the idea of becoming a musician, but his parents expected him to become a lawyer. He began a law course at St Petersburg University in 1901, but was unsuited to it. He was already spending more time on music studies than law when his father died in 1902. In 1905 the university was temporarily closed in the wake of political disturbances and Stravinsky was prevented from taking his law finals.

With only a half-course diploma, his way was open to pursue music. He was advised by Rimsky-Korsakov, the leading Russian composer of the day, not to enter the St Petersburg Conservatoire, because of his age – he was now 24. Instead, Rimsky-Korsakov gave him twice-weekly private lessons and became a second father to him.

Stravinsky's career as a composer falls into several distinct stylistic phases, almost as if he was several separate composers. His first phase (the Russian Period) was, understandably, as a composer of ballet scores. He became famous for three ballets written for Sergei Diaghilev, the impresario, and performed by the *Ballets Russes*. These were *The Firebird* (1910), *Petrushka* (1911) and *The Rite of Spring* (1913). These were dazzling early masterpieces. *The Rite of Spring* caused a riot at its first performance, an event that put Stravinsky firmly on the map as a musical revolutionary.

The later of these works were written while Stravinsky and his young family were staying in Switzerland; a pattern of Bohemian mobility was being established. They were in Switzerland when World War I broke out and were unable to return to Russia; in fact Stravinsky would not return there for 50 years.

There were also financial difficulties. Apparently Diaghilev did not abide by the terms of their agreement, and Russia was not party to the international Berne convention on royalties, so Stravinsky received no payments. Stravinsky was forced to seek patronage. He asked Werner Reinhart for help, and Reinhart financed the composition of *The Soldier's Tale* (1918) and some performances of Stravinsky's chamber music.

Then, after the trauma of World War I and a move to France, Stravinsky's music entered a more formal, neoclassical phase. He even used the traditional forms of the 18th and 19th centuries, the symphony, the *concerto grosso*, the fugue. The surface of this music was often austere, but concealing a high intensity of emotion. Conscious of the need to earn money, Stravinsky entered an agreement with the Pleyel company, to arrange his own music so that it could be played on the Pleyela, the Pleyel's pianola, which worked on the barrel organ principle.

"To listen is an effort, and just to hear is no merit. A duck hears also."

Stravinsky was able to make full use of the piano keyboard, because any number of notes could be played at once. These pianola versions were useful, in that many orchestras found Stravinsky's music beyond their capabilities. The early ballet scores all became available in Pleyela versions, which people could play in their own homes. But even in the 1920s Stravinsky needed financial support; this was supplied, anonymously, by the conductor Leopold Stokowski.

Stravinsky was still in Paris in 1934, the unhappiest year of his life. His wife had tuberculosis, which infected him and their daughter; he recovered after five months in hospital, but his daughter died. His mother also died while he was in hospital. His wife died in 1939.

When World War II broke out, Stravinsky emigrated to America, having already agreed to write a symphony for the Chicago Symphony Orchestra and to lecture at Harvard. He lived for a long time in Los Angeles, which he found culturally richer than Paris; he was able to make friends with the musicians Otto Klemperer, George Balanchine, Arthur Rubinstein and the writers Thomas Mann, W. H. Auden, Christopher Isherwood and Dylan Thomas.

Schoenberg lived nearby, but they were not friends. Schoenberg referred to Stravinsky derisively as 'Mr Modernsky'. After World War II Stravinsky (belatedly) adopted Schoenberg's 12-note system; significantly he waited until after Schoenberg's death.

Agon (1957) was the first work he wrote to include a 12-note row. But still he retained the rhythmic energy of his earlier pieces. He received a warning from the Boston police for his re-arrangement of *The Star-Spangled Banner*: it was the new ('wrong') harmonies that were causing distress.

Stravinsky wrote several books, mostly with a collaborator. His 1936 autobiography, *Chronicles of My Life*, expressed the view that 'music is, by its very nature, essentially powerless to express anything at all'. He can scarcely have believed that, but he liked to be the *enfant terrible*, always provocative and shocking.

His claim to have had an affair with Coco Chanel was almost certainly untrue, and similarly designed to shock. In the 1940s and 1950s he published several books of 'conversations' with Robert Craft. In 1962 he went back to Leningrad (St Petersburg) in response to an invitation to conduct a series of concerts. While in Russia, he met Khachaturian and Shostakovich.

When he died in New York in 1971, Stravinsky had experimented with and extended most of the musical styles of the 20th century. He absorbed many influences, from Russian folk songs on, and his music itself became a great influence on other composers. He had an unquenchable curiosity about art, literature and life – not just music. In politics, he was a reactionary right-winger – he loved the Tsars and he loved Mussolini, at least in 1930.

He made a range of technical innovations in music, especially in rhythm and harmony. But perhaps the most remarkable feature of his music is its perpetual changes of style, while yet retaining a distinctive personal identity. From first to last it is Stravinsky.

> **"People are taught to have too much respect for music, they should be taught to love it instead."**

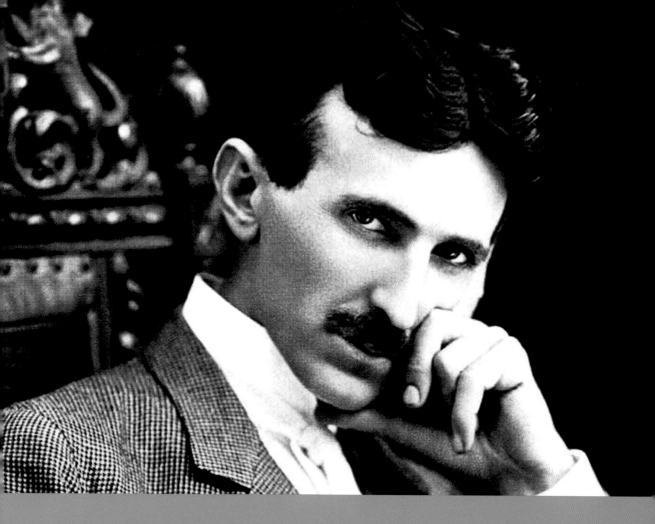

NIKOLA TESLA

The Man Who Made The Modern World

QUOTE

"Invention is the most important product of man's creative brain."

BIOGRAPHY

NAME: Nikola Tesla

BORN: July 10, 1856
Smiljan, Croatia

DIED: January 7, 1943 (Aged 86)
New York City, New York,
United States

NATIONALITY: Serbian American

OCCUPATION: Inventor, Electrical
Engineer, Physicist

Born in the small Croatian village of Smiljan at midnight on July 10, 1856, Nikola Tesla was ethnically a Serb. Tesla's father, Milutin, was an Orthodox priest and his mother, Djouka, never learned to read, but could memorize epic Serbian poems and long passages of the Bible. Tesla attributed his phenomenal eidetic memory to her.

At school, in 1870, legend has it, that Tesla worked out calculus equations in his head and completed a four-year course in three, graduating when he was 17. In 1875, he took up a scholarship at the Polytechnic in Graz, Austria. By 1880, he was studying in Prague where his interest in electricity grew and he applied for a job with one of Thomas Edison's agents who was setting up an electric telephone exchange in Budapest.

Tesla may have also found inspiration visiting the works of Ganz and Company in Budapest. Electrical engineers there had found that a metal ball placed on top of a alternating current transformer revolved in a rotating magnetic field.

In 1881, Tesla was taken on by the Edison Organization first to work in Budapest and then Paris in 1882, designing and making improvements to electrical equipment all over Europe. In June 1884, Tesla relocated to New York City and was hired by Edison himself.

Tesla's work for Edison began with simple electrical engineering and quickly progressed to solving some of the company's most difficult problems. But the two men clashed over their electrical beliefs. The entire Edison Company was built around DC electricity whereas AC electricity was fundamental to all Tesla's work. In 1885, their stormy relationship came to a head with an argument over the non-payment of a promised bonus, and Tesla resigned.

However in 1887, with new investors, New York attorney Charles Peck, and Alfred Brown of the Western Union company, Tesla set up his first laboratory in Manhattan. By May 1888, he had built and patented his first Alternating Current induction motor, based on a rotating magnetic field, agreeing a 50-50 profit share with the investors.

Soon after, Tesla demonstrated his AC motor at the recently formed American Institute of Electrical Engineers. His work impressed the assembled electrical pioneers including engineers from Thomas Edison's main rival in electrical power distribution – Westinghouse Electric, who had been developing a similar motor. In July 1888, George Westinghouse licensed Tesla's American patents for the induction motor and transformer designs. The terms included Tesla working as a consultant for Westinghouse. Westinghouse's promotion of AC power distribution led him into a bitter long-lasting confrontation with Edison and his DC power system.

"The scientists of today think deeply instead of clearly. One must be sane to think clearly, but one can think deeply and be quite insane."

In 1893, Westinghouse Electric won the contract to electrify the World's Fair, staged in Chicago to celebrate the 400th anniversary of Christopher Columbus arriving in the New World in 1492. Also known as the Columbian Exposition, Westinghouse and Tesla lit up the Fair in a blaze of electric light and flashing signs to prove to America that AC power was safe and reliable. It was a turning point and generated massive publicity for the company and AC power. In an action-packed spectacular show, Tesla wowed the crowd with dazzling electrical effects including magically lighting up wireless lamps, and dramatically running high voltages through his own body. He also mystified his audience with his Egg of Columbus showpiece – the metal ball spinning in a rotating magnetic field, that he had first seen back at the Ganz works in Budapest, 12 years before.

Based on the great success of AC at the World's Fair in 1893, the International Niagara Commission awarded the contract to Westinghouse to build the new hydro-electric power generator at Niagara Falls using Tesla's polyphase AC system. But construction of the first power station at Niagara was a headache from the start and took 5 years to complete. The outlay was huge and no-one knew whether it would work as the plans lay principally in Tesla's imagination. However, with teamwork and much practical input from the brother and sister team of Westinghouse electrical engineers, Benjamin and Bertha Lamme, the first power reached Buffalo, 25 miles (40 km) away, on November 16, 1896. Within a few years, power lines ran from Niagara Falls as far as New York City. Broadway was ablaze with lights and even Thomas Edison converted to alternating current.

In 1899, Tesla set up a laboratory in Colorado Springs. Over a mile (1.6 km) above sea level, Colorado Springs is situated near the base of one of the most famous American mountains, Pike's Peak, on the eastern edge of the Southern Rocky Mountains. More importantly as far as Tesla was concerned, Colorado Springs is also one of the most active lightning strike areas in the United States. This natural phenomenon helped him produce 135 ft high powered artificial lightning bolts and thunder that could be heard 15 miles away.

Around Tesla's lab, sparks jumped from the ground, light bulbs lit up even when turned off and electrified grass glowed blue with the luminous electric field of St Elmo's fire. But continual power outages caused by Tesla's experiments short circuiting local power stations meant that the good people of Colorado Springs soon tired of Tesla's thunder and lightning experiments and he was unceremoniously asked to leave town.

But the Colorado experiments were just a prelude, for Tesla's central tele-communications hub in 1904, known as Wardenclyffe near Shoreham, Long Island. From this facility, Tesla hoped to demonstrate wireless transmission of electrical energy across the Atlantic. But his *pièce de résistance* soon dissolved into a hugely expensive folly as he asked his investor J.P. Morgan for more and more extravagant funding causing Morgan eventually to pull the plug on the project. Tesla's great unfinished masterpiece crumbled into decay and was eventually torn down by the US government during World War I.

Tesla's theories on the possibility of transmission by radio waves go back as far as lectures and demonstrations in 1893. He is now acknowledged to have beaten Guglielmo Marconi to the invention of the radio. Indeed, he spoke of his world system of wireless transmission the year before Marconi transmitted the first radio signal across the Atlantic. His Tesla Coil, invented in 1891, is widely used in radio and television sets, and other electronic equipment. He developed electric motors, generators, X-rays, fluorescent tubes, remote control and radar. However, many of his inventions are unacknowledged because he was so busy developing new ideas he never bothered to patent them.

On January 7, 1943, Tesla, 86, died of a heart attack, alone in Room 3327 of the New Yorker Hotel – he always insisted his room number be divisible by 3. Despite having sold his AC electricity patents, Tesla died impoverished and in debt.

Nikola Tesla is the man who made the modern world. Not only did he invent many of the electrical devices we take for granted today, but he also had a future vision, much of which has become reality long after his death. He would have felt vindicated by our contemporary world of wireless transmission. But Tesla was not just a visionary who delivered theory. He was a practical man who pioneered alternating current that made it possible to transmit electricity over long distances, allowing electrical appliances to be powered by remote power stations, rather than a power station on every street corner as the earlier direct current system envisaged.

Nikola Tesla surrounded by artificial
lightning generated by a giant Tesla
coil, Colorado Springs, 1899.

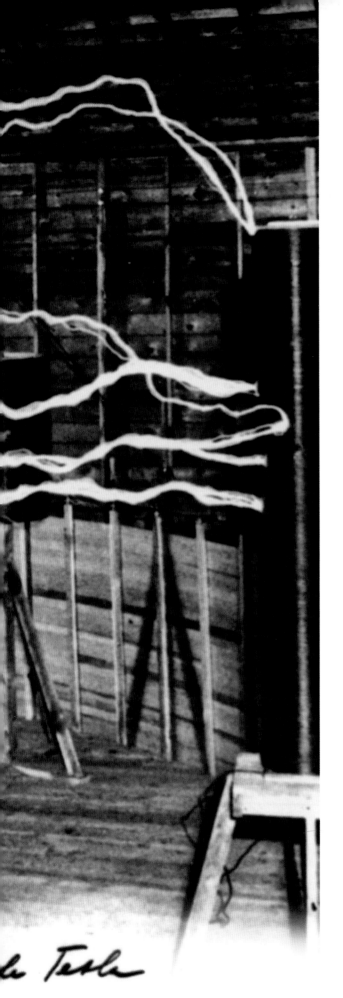

Although he was never awarded a Nobel Prize, three Nobel laureates lauded him as 'one of the outstanding intellects of the world'. He appeared on the cover of *Time* magazine and the unit of magnetic induction, a minor planet, a crater on the moon, an electric car company and an airport are all named after him.

Otherwise, with his talk of death rays and communication from other planets, his image endures as that of the quintessential mad scientist. But he was far from mad. He was one of the towering figures of the modern age, arguably more influential to our everyday lives than Einstein, Stravinsky or Picasso. Seventy-one years after his death, he deserves to be better known and recognized as one of the brilliant minds of the last 100 years.

"Let the future tell the truth, and evaluate each one according to his work and accomplishments. The present is theirs; the future, for which I have really worked, is mine."

ALAN TURING

Turning the Tide of War

"A computer would deserve to be called intelligent if it could deceive a human into believing that it was human."

BIOGRAPHY

NAME: Alan Mathison Turing

BORN: June 23, 1912
Maida Vale, London, England,
United Kingdom

DIED: June 7, 1954 (Aged 41)
Wilmslow, Cheshire, England,
United Kingdom

NATIONALITY: British

OCCUPATION: Mathematician, logician,
cryptanalyst, computer
scientist

The brilliant English mathematician Alan Turing was born in 1912. His father, Julius, was a member of the Indian Civil Service and his mother, Ethel, was the daughter of the chief engineer of the Madras Railways. Alan was conceived in India, but his parents wanted him to grow up in England so they returned to Maida Vale, in north London where he was born. His parents continued to shuttle between England and India, leaving Alan and his elder brother John with a retired Army couple. Alan began to show signs of high intelligence at an early age, and many of his teachers recognized it.

At 14 years old he went to Sherborne School, an independent boys school, located in the town of Sherborne in north-west Dorset, England. His first day there, in 1926, coincided with the General Strike, so there was no public transport. But Alan was determined not to miss the opening day of term and rode 60 miles on a bicycle, on his own, from the city of Southampton to the school.

By the age of 16, Alan Turing was not only looking at Einstein's Theory of Relativity, he *understood* it, and was able to extrapolate Einstein's questioning of Newton's Laws of Motion from a passage in which this was not openly stated.

Alan Turing went to King's College, Cambridge, where he graduated with a first-class degree in mathematics in 1934. The following year, when he was still only 22, he was elected a Fellow of the University in recognition of the brilliance of a dissertation in which he proved the central limit theorem. He did not then know that it had already been proved in 1922.

Turing devised a method for problem-solving by using simple hypothetical devices that became known as Turing Machines. These were in effect a new and relatively straightforward method for computation. In 1936 he developed the idea of a 'universal machine', which would be able to compute anything computable. Turing Machines are still studied in theory of computation. Turing was excited by his discovery, and disappointed by the general lack of interest in it.

He spent from 1936 to 1938 at Princeton, New Jersey, USA studying cryptology and built three out of four stages of a electro-mechanical binary multiplier, a primitive type of computer. In his PhD thesis from Princeton he supplemented his Turing Machines with 'oracles', which allowed an examination of problems that were beyond solving by a Turing Machine.

> *"A man provided with paper, pencil, and rubber, and subject to strict discipline, is in effect a universal machine."*

Turing cannot have been easy to teach: he displayed many of the classic symptoms of Asperger's syndrome. At this time he started part-time work with the British Government Code and Cypher School (GCCS) at Bletchley Park, and while he was working there he acquired a reputation for eccentricity. To ward off attacks of hay fever, he would cycle to work wearing a gas mask. Logical, but odd. He was a long-distance runner and occasionally he ran the 40 miles into central London for high-level meetings. He was the archetypal 'mad boffin'.

Once World War II started, the code-breaking work intensified. For a time he was in charge of Hut 8, the section responsible for analyzing German navy codes. He devised techniques for code-breaking, including the Bombe, an electromechanical machine (in effect an early computer, for which he designed the specifications) that was able to find settings for the German Enigma code.

The Enigma cypher was the backbone of German military and intelligence communications that was thought to be unbreakable. Enigma's complexity was indeed bewildering. The odds against anyone being able to break Enigma were a staggering 150 million million million to one.

The Bombe searched for possible settings for a particular Enigma message, starting from a suitable 'crib', which was a fragment of probable text. The bombe tried out as many as 10^{19} possible combinations based on the crib, detected when a contradiction occurred and ruled that setting out; then it went on to try the next.

Most settings led to contradictions, leaving a small number to be explored in detail. Turing's method was a way of reducing the scale of the decoding problem. The first of these computers was set up in March 1940, and by the end of the war there were over 200 of them in operation.

Turing was responsible for other, less well-known, security-related inventions during the war, including a portable secure voice-scrambler code-named Delilah. When the war was over, Turing worked at the National Physical Laboratory, and it was there that he designed the first stored-program computer, the ACE.

In 1948, he went to Manchester University to join the Computing Laboratory, where he assisted in the development of the Manchester computers. He also explored the idea of artificial intelligence and proposed an experiment which became known as the Turing test, a standard by which a machine could be judged 'intelligent'. A computer can be said to 'think' if a human interrogator cannot tell, through dialogue, whether he is talking to a person or a machine.

Disaster struck in 1952, however, when Alan Turing was convicted of homosexual activity, at that time illegal in Britain. MI6 had known about his private life as early as 1944, but the head of MI6, Stewart Menzies, regarded Turing's war work as taking precedence. By 1952, Turing was no longer seen as indispensable – the protection was withdrawn. He was charged, found guilty and convicted.

He agreed to be treated with oestrogen injections as an alternative to being sent to prison. Two years later, aged 41, he committed suicide by eating a poisoned apple. It is often said that this is the origin of the Apple Computers logo. Steve Jobs denied it, 'It isn't true, but, God, we wish it were.'

On December 24, 2013, after many years of campaigning on his behalf, Alan Turing was granted a posthumous royal pardon, 61 years after his conviction. The pardon was issued under the Royal Prerogative of Mercy after a request by Justice Minister Chris Grayling, who said, 'Dr Alan Turing was an exceptional man with a brilliant mind. His later life was overshadowed by his conviction for homosexual activity, a sentence we would now consider unjust and discriminatory and which has now been repealed. He deserves to be remembered and recognized for his fantastic contribution to the war effort and his legacy to science. A pardon from the Queen is a fitting tribute to an exceptional man.'

Hugh Alexander, who became head of Hut 8 during Turing's 1942–43 visit to America to help set up code-breaking there, also paid tribute to Turing's genius. 'There should be no question in anyone's mind that Turing's work was the biggest factor in Hut 8's success. In the early days he was the only cryptographer who thought the problem worth tackling and not only was he primarily responsible for the main theoretical work within the Hut but he also shared the chief credit for the invention of the Bombe … Many of us in Hut 8 felt that the magnitude of Turing's contribution was never fully realized by the outside world.'

The historian Asa Briggs was one of the code-breakers who worked alongside Alan Turing. He said, 'You needed exceptional talent, you needed genius at Bletchley and Turing's was that genius.'

"Mathematical reasoning may be regarded as the combination of intuition and ingenuity."

ANDY WARHOL

The Man Behind the Painted Smile

QUOTE

"If you look at a thing long enough, it loses all of its meaning."

BIOGRAPHY

NAME: Andrew Warhola

BORN: August 6, 1928
Pittsburgh, Pennsylvania,
United States

DIED: February 22, 1987 (Aged 58)
New York City, New York,
United States

NATIONALITY: American

OCCUPATION: Artist

The controversial American artist Andy Warhol was born in Pittsburgh, Pennsylvania to a working-class migrant family from Slovakia in 1928. His father was Ondrej Varchola, who arrived in America in 1914; his mother Julia joined him in 1921. Ondrej was a coal-miner. The young Andy suffered poor health. He had chorea, which caused involuntary movements of the extremities and blotchy skin, and he was often bedridden. At school his physical peculiarity made him an outcast.

Warhol showed a talent for art early on. He studied commercial art at the Carnegie Institute of Technology in Pittsburgh, moving from there to start a career in magazine illustration and advertising in New York. As the record industry developed, with the introduction of vinyl, hi-fi and stereo recordings, Andy Warhol was hired by RCA Records to design record sleeves and promotional material.

Early in his career, Warhol started using the silk-screen print-making process. He developed a technique of applying ink to paper then blotting the ink while wet – it produced a distinctive style of image. His work then and later shows a casual approach; he allowed chance flaws, smudges and smears to appear in his work. Imperfection was his hallmark. He said, 'When you do something exactly wrong, you always turn up something.'

Warhol started exhibiting his work in the 1950s, and his first one-man gallery exhibition came in 1962 in Los Angeles. In the 1960s, Warhol started painting iconic American objects and people – Coca-Cola bottles, Campbell's soup cans, Marilyn Monroe, Elvis Presley. He set up his studio, The Factory, where he gathered round him a fluid community of artists, musicians, film-makers and writers. Suddenly Warhol's work was extremely popular, extremely commercial, and controversial.

Warhol was intrigued by American culture and American society, and by the way iconic objects were great levellers. The richest consumers bought the same things as the poorest. Warhol said, 'You know that the President drinks Coca-Cola, Liz Taylor drinks Coca-Cola, and just think, you can drink Coca-Cola, too … All the cokes are the same and all the cokes are good. Liz Taylor knows it, the President knows it, the bum knows it, and you know it.'

At a conference at the Museum of Modern Art in New York in 1962, speakers attacked Warhol for selling out to consumerism – they said the way he was embracing the market culture was a scandal. Warhol was at the centre of a major cultural shift towards the lowest common factor, and those who didn't like it have called it 'dumbing-down' – and condemned it accordingly.

At the 1964 exhibition significantly called *The American Supermarket*, six pop artists produced everything in it – produce, canned goods, wall posters. Warhol's painting of a can of Campbell's soup was on sale at $1,500, and autographed soup cans were on sale for $6. Warhol and his fellow-artists were confronting the public with the fundamental question, 'What is art? And what is not art? And what is the difference?'

"I'd prefer to remain a mystery."

As early as the 1950s, when he was an ad illustrator, Warhol was using assistants. In the 1960s, when he was producing fine art rather than commercial art, he went on using assistants, to increase his rate of production. Warhol's main collaborator at The Factory in the 1960s was Gerard Malanga. This collaboration has remained a central and controversial conundrum with Warhol's work. Is a piece of work that we know was produced by someone else, to Warhol's specifications, by Andy Warhol or by someone else? Does his signature on someone else's work make it his work? These are questions art dealers today have to deal with.

Also controversial was the way Warhol groomed a band of followers. He called these Bohemian eccentrics 'superstars'. They included Joe Dallesandro, Edie Sedgewick, Ultra Violet, Holly Woodlawn, Jackie Curtis and Candy Darling. They took part in Warhol's Factory films.

One of those at the fringe of this community was Valerie Solanas. She wrote a feminist attack on men. She had given Warhol a film script she had worked on and when she called at The Factory on June 3, 1968 to ask for it back she was asked to leave; it seems the script had been mislaid. She came back with a gun and shot Andy Warhol, who was seriously wounded. He eventually recovered, but went on suffering the effects of the injury for the rest of his life.

When arrested, Valerie Solanas explained that Warhol 'had too much control over my life'. She was given a three-year sentence. Access to The Factory was more rigorously controlled after that, as Warhol became more nervous and security-conscious. The incident was overshadowed in the press and on television by the coincidental assassination of Robert F. Kennedy. Warhol said about the shooting, 'People sometimes say that the way things happen in movies is unreal, but actually it's the way things happen in life that's unreal … When things really do happen to you, it's like watching television – you don't feel anything.'

Warhol's public life was quieter in the 1970s. His creative life was just as busy, and just as commercially oriented. He spent a lot of his time lining up rich patrons for portrait commissions: the Shah of Iran and his wife the Empress Farah, Mick Jagger, John Lennon, Liza Minnelli, Brigitte Bardot. In 1975, he said, 'Making money is art.'

In 1979, Warhol and his friend Stuart Pivar set up the New York Academy of Art. In the 1980s, he cultivated a circle of younger New York artists. The criticism that he was superficial and only interested in making money continued unabated until his death, and after his death. But some critics have started to re-assess. Now that a couple of decades separate us from Warhol's career, some see with hindsight that his superficiality and commerciality are 'the most brilliant mirror of our times'.

Somehow, Warhol saw straight to the heart of American culture, especially the pop culture of the 1970s. Andy Warhol's sayings and writings are of a piece with this, and refreshingly frank. 'I love Los Angeles. I love Hollywood. They're so beautiful. Everything's plastic, but I love plastic.' He admired glitz, glamour, success and money – and achieved all of them, along with, perhaps, the disorientation of American popular culture. After his death, it took Sotheby's nine days to auction his possessions, which fetched over $20 million.

"Making money is art and working is art and good business is the best art."

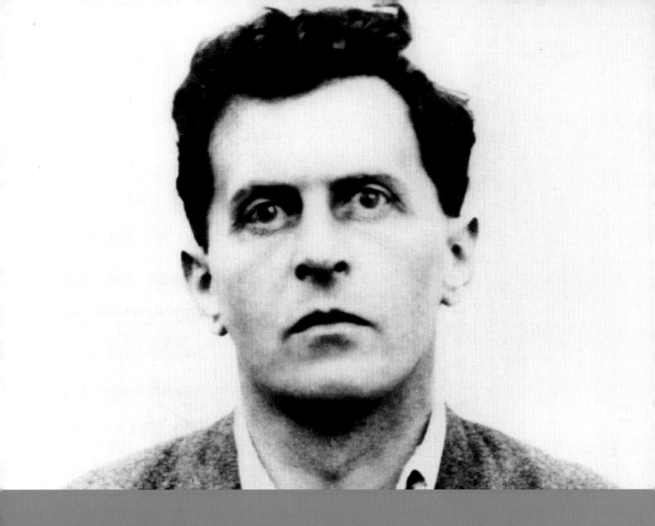

LUDWIG WITTGENSTEIN

Unlocking the Philosophy of the Mind

QUOTE ━━

"Philosophy is like trying to open a safe with a combination lock: each little adjustment of the dials seems to achieve nothing, only when everything is in place does the door open."

BIOGRAPHY ━━━━━━━━━━━━━━━━━━━━━━━━━━━━━━━━━━━━

NAME:	Ludwig Josef Johann Wittgenstein	**NATIONALITY:**	Austrian-British
		OCCUPATION:	Philosopher
BORN:	April 26, 1889 Vienna, Austria-Hungary		
DIED:	April 29, 1951 (Aged 62) Cambridge, England, United Kingdom		

The Austrian-British philosopher Ludwig Wittgenstein was unusual in being born into a phenomenally rich family. His father, Karl, was an industrialist with a virtual monopoly on steel in Austria. The Wittgensteins were the second richest family in the Habsburg Empire, after the Rothschilds.

The family lived in an intense environment in the Wittgenstein palace at the centre of Vienna's cultural life. Karl was a patron of the arts, regularly inviting Brahms and Mahler to give concerts in his palace. Karl expected his sons to become industrialists. They were educated at home in the subjects of Karl's choice, to prepare them for industry. Karl was a harsh perfectionist, lacking in empathy – depression and neurosis ran through the family.

Three of Karl's sons, Ludwig's brothers, committed suicide and Ludwig, the youngest, also thought of killing himself. Ludwig told a friend that when Bertrand Russell had first encouraged him in his philosophy, in 1912, it had brought to a close nine years of loneliness. Russell was nevertheless so anxious about Wittgenstein's state of mind that he predicted Wittgenstein would kill himself by 1914.

Wittgenstein attended the same school as Adolf Hitler, they were there at the same time and they were exactly the same age; it is probable that the two boys knew one another.

Wittgenstein's further education consisted of mechanical engineering in Berlin, where he started in 1906 and gained a diploma in 1908. Then he went to Manchester, England to study for a doctorate. He was fleetingly interested in aeronautics; he aspired to design and fly his own plane. While conducting this research he became interested in the foundations of mathematics, particularly after reading Bertrand Russell on the subject.

His interest switched from aeronautics to mathematics and logic. He visited Gottlob Frege, the German mathematician, logician and philosopher, at Jena in Germany to show him an essay he had written on the philosophy of mathematics and logic and ask whether it was worth pursuing. He

commented later that Frege 'absolutely wiped the floor' with him. He felt depressed, but at the end Frege said, 'You must come again.' Wittgenstein hoped Frege would teach him, but Frege told him he should go to Cambridge University, England to study with Bertrand Russell.

In October 1911, Wittgenstein turned up unannounced at Russell's rooms in Cambridge. He attended Russell's lectures and soon dominated them; Russell's lectures were often attended by only four students, so Wittgenstein was very noticeable. Then Wittgenstein started following Russell around, for yet more philosophy. Russell felt he was being stalked. But when he read Wittgenstein's essays, he came to believe that Wittgenstein was a genius.

Three months later, Russell wrote, 'I feel he will solve the problems I am too old to solve. He is *the* young man one hopes for.' Soon Russell was seeking Wittgenstein's view of his own work saying, 'He has more passion about philosophy than I have; his avalanches make mine seem mere snowballs … He says every morning he begins his work with hope, and every evening he ends in despair.'

Wittgenstein joined the Moral Sciences Club, a Cambridge philosophy club, where he became the problem member: he never gave others a chance to speak. Another Austrian philosopher, Karl Popper, was invited to speak on 'Are there philosophical problems?' Popper thought philosophical problems were real, not just linguistic puzzles, as Wittgenstein argued. Wittgenstein waved a poker at Popper, demanding an example of a moral rule from him. Popper offered 'Not to threaten visiting speakers with pokers', and Wittgenstein had to be disarmed by Russell.

"A philosopher who is not taking part in discussions is like a boxer who never goes into the ring."

John Maynard Keynes invited him to join the Cambridge literary intellectual group the Apostles, but Wittgenstein did not appreciate their light-hearted banter. Lytton Strachey, the English writer, a prominent member of the Apostles, unpleasantly referred to Wittgenstein as Herr Sinckel-Winckel, who didn't get the jokes and took everything too continuously seriously.

During World War I, Wittgenstein volunteered for service in the Austro-Hungarian army, and in 1916 was involved in heavy fighting on the Russian front. He won a medal for his service against the British. In 1917 he was back at the Russian front, winning more medals. He kept notes throughout, including contemptuous remarks about the other soldiers. He read Tolstoy's *The Gospel in Brief*. Russell said he came back from the war a different man, deeply mystical and ascetic.

In 1918, he finished *Tractatus*. The publisher rejected it. This blow was compounded by the deaths, in quick succession, of his uncle, his brother Kurt and his lover, David Pinsent. He was sent to the Italian front, where he was captured and spent nine months in a prisoner-of-war camp. In 1919, when he returned exhausted to Vienna, he talked of suicide and decided to give his fortune to his siblings to become a teacher.

In 1920 he became a primary school teacher at a remote village, where he disliked the other teachers and found the villagers 'odious and base'. In the classroom he was short-tempered, hitting both boys and girls when they made mistakes, knocking out an 11-year-old after hitting him three times.

Meanwhile, *Tractatus* was published with an introduction by Russell. As on other previous occasions, Wittgenstein was less than grateful and bit the helping hand. He criticized Russell for misunderstanding his work; he thought Russell glib. *Tractatus* was to show the link between language and the world. Language has a logical structure that sets the limits on what can meaningfully be said; the limits of language are the limits of philosophy.

But much of philosophy contains attempts to say the unsayable. The unsayable may not be nonsense, but anything said about it must be. Wittgenstein apologized for the shortness of the book (75 pages), but that was all he had to say. He further reduced what he had to say to just seven statements, and the most famous is the seventh: 'Whereof one cannot speak, thereof one must be silent.'

When the German Third Reich annexed Austria in 1938, Wittgenstein applied for British citizenship. He had earlier admitted that he had *one* Jewish grandparent, now he claimed *three*. He became Professor of Philosophy at Cambridge, in 1939, and became a British citizen soon afterwards. He was daunting as a lecturer. He spoke with great force, and his presence was described as 'imperial' and 'frightening'.

During his lifetime, Wittgenstein published very little: one book review, one article and the *Tractatus Logico-Philosophicus*, which was only 75 pages long. But after his death came *Philosophical Investigations*, and when it was published in 1953 it was hailed as the most important philosophical book of the century. It was seen as a 'cross-over' masterpiece that appealed across disciplinary boundaries. Bertrand Russell described him as 'the most perfect example I have ever known of genius as traditionally conceived, passionate, profound, intense, and dominating.'

"A man will be imprisoned in a room with a door that's unlocked and opens inward; as long as it does not occur to him to pull rather than push."

FLOSSIE WONG-STAAL

A Passion for Making Discoveries

QUOTE

*"You have to realize that you're in for a long haul.
Eureka moments are few and far between."*

BIOGRAPHY

NAME: Yee Ching Wong-Staal

BORN: August 27, 1947
Guangzhou, Guangdong, China

NATIONALITY: American

OCCUPATION: Molecular biologist and
virologist, AIDS research
pioneer

Flossie Wong-Staal is one of the world's leading experts in viruses. She was one of the scientists involved in the discovery of the human immuno-deficiency virus (HIV) which causes AIDS. Yet her high achievements in science did not come easily to her.

She was born in mainland China with the name Yee Ching Wong. Her father was a businessman. She fled with her family in 1952 to Hong Kong, where she attended a girls' Catholic school. Girls at this school who achieved high grades were encouraged to take science courses. This was not her natural interest but, contrary to her expectations, she was very good at mathematics and science and came to enjoy science in particular.

As was the custom in those days, the nuns at the school encouraged the girls to adopt an English name. Her father did not have any command of English, and picked a name for her out of the newspaper, where there were reports of Typhoon Flossie, which had struck Hong Kong the previous week. So she was called Flossie. Later she told *Discover* magazine, 'I used to be embarrassed by [it]. Now I'm trying to change the image of the name.'

When she was growing up there was no real role model for her. Her father was a businessman, but he was a man; her mother was a conventional Chinese home-maker and all the other women in the family were full-time housewives too. No-one in the Wong family had ever gone to university, but Flossie was enthusiastically supported when it was suggested that higher education would help her. In 1965, she went to America to study science at the University of California at Los Angeles. She gained a BSc in bacteriology in 1968 and went on to take a doctorate in molecular biology in 1972.

While working on the research for her doctorate, Flossie Wong married and became Flossie Wong-Staal. In 1973, she began working at the National Cancer Institute at Bethesda in Maryland. There she studied retro-viruses with AIDS pioneer Robert Gallo. Retro-viruses are the family of viruses to which HIV belongs, but at that time the existence of HIV was unknown.

The AIDS epidemic was under way, and researchers were working feverishly to isolate and identify the cause of the many illnesses that together make up the syndrome. Flossie Wong-Staal was at the forefront of the search for the cause of AIDS. She was on the National Cancer Institute AIDS research team with Robert Gallo and other co-workers, when HIV was identified in 1983. As often happens in science, the discovery was made simultaneously elsewhere, by a French researcher, Montagnier. The discovery that HIV was the cause of AIDS was a major breakthrough.

In 1985, Wong-Staal undertook the first cloning of the HIV virus, and it was her initiative that led to the first genetic mapping of the virus. This in turn led eventually to the development of tests that enabled the screening of patients and potential blood donors – well before they actually developed AIDS. So Flossie Wong-Staal's work had a major effect on limiting the spread of AIDS, and reducing the number of people infected with AIDS.

In 1990, her work was recognized, when the US Institute for Scientific Information named Flossie Wong-Staal as the top woman scientist of the previous decade, and the fourth highest achieving woman under the age of 45. She went back to the University of California, San Diego, to carry on with her AIDS research and in 1994, San Diego set up a new Center for Aids Research with Wong-Staal as its chairman. There she worked towards finding a vaccine against HIV and therapies for those suffering from AIDS. A cure for AIDS seemed a long way off.

Dr Wong-Staal and her team at UCSD worked in collaboration with five other research institutions across the USA, in particular to find a way of preventing HIV from reproducing itself in infected people. A promising area of her research seemed to be in gene therapy. She also worked with pharmaceutical companies to develop drugs that might be able to short-circuit or stall the AIDS reproductive cycle.

One of her techniques was to obtain a cold virus that will imitate HIV; the resulting vaccine might then be administered through a nose spray. She said, 'Our goal is to make a virus as similar to the real one as possible, but to make sure there's no risk of introducing its dangerous genes into an uninfected population.' She attempted to make the outer layer of proteins surrounding HIV larger.

Another initiative was to create a molecule called the octamer, which responds five hundred times faster than the normal HIV cell. Further techniques included research into the development of a vaccine from the complete virus, though there are inherent dangers in giving people 'more' HIV.

Commenting on the fact that the uniqueness of the HIV virus still poses major roadblocks to finding a viable vaccine for AIDS, Dr Wong-Staal said, 'HIV differs in some major ways from most other viruses. First of all, as a retrovirus, it integrates its genetic information into the person's DNA and can remain dormant during drug therapy, even when offspring viruses are not being made.'

She retired from UCSD in 2002 to co-found the Immusol company, and took on the role of Chief Scientific Officer. Immusol changed its name to iTherX Pharmaceuticals in 2007, when it turned into a drug development company with a focus on Hepatitis C; she is currently its Chief Scientific Officer.

Wong-Staal, as co-discoverer of HIV, has been named one of the 50 most extraordinary women scientists. In 2007, a list compiled by *The Daily Telegraph* featured Dr Wong-Staal as number 32 in the 'Top 100 Living Geniuses'. An outstanding feature of her work has been persistence over the long-haul, her determination to carry on trying. This is reminiscent of the painstaking work of another brilliant woman scientist, with whom we began the book, Jocelyn Bell. This is a very special type of genius.

"You need to have a passion for making discoveries."

FRANK LLOYD WRIGHT

Building the 20th Century

QUOTE

"Simplicity and repose are the qualities that measure the true value of any work of art."

BIOGRAPHY

NAME: Frank Lincoln Wright

BORN: June 8, 1867
Richland Center, Wisconsin,
United States

DIED: April 9, 1959 (Aged 91)
Phoenix, Arizona, United States

NATIONALITY: American

OCCUPATION: Architect, interior designer

Frank Lincoln Wright was born at Richland Center, a farming community in Wisconsin, USA on June 8, 1867. His father William Wright was married to Anna Lloyd Jones, but the couple later divorced in 1885 when the family was living in Madison, Wisconsin. Sixteen-year-old Frank changed his middle name from Lincoln to Lloyd to support his mother and pay tribute to her family.

Frank Lloyd Wright studied civil engineering at Wisconsin University, after his life had been changed by a singular event in 1882 – the collapse of a newly-built wing of the Wisconsin State Capitol building in Madison. This spectacular catastrophe contributed greatly to his rising interest in construction and architecture. The engineering failure of the building pointed the way for his future resolve to apply top quality engineering principles to all his architectural design work. He was already a man on a mission, when he arrived in Chicago seeking employment in 1888.

He was hired as a draftsman by the architectural firm of Joseph Lynman Silsbee, but soon aspired for greater challenges. After less than a year with Silsbee he left to work for a more progressive Chicago firm of architects, Adler & Sullivan. He started as an apprentice, but soon became the young protégé of one of the partners, Louis H. Sullivan.

In 1888, Louis Henry Sullivan was one of the most influential architects in Chicago and is often referred to as the father of the skyscraper. The Auditorium Theater in Chicago is among his most famous surviving works. Sullivan influenced the young Frank Lloyd Wright profoundly during the six years that Wright spent as his draftsman and Sullivan's geometric styling is clearly reflected in Wright's work.

In 1890, Wright had risen to head draftsman responsible for the residential design work for Sullivan's entire office. But despite overtime and a loan from Sullivan, Wright was always short of funds and started taking on freelance work to supplement his income.

By 1893, he had designed at least nine sought-after 'bootleg' houses in Chicago which were clearly in the Sullivan style that Wright had made his own. Unfortunately, the houses were so distinctive that they drew attention to Wright's freelance ventures and Louis Sullivan fired him for breach of contract. It would be another 12 years before the two men spoke to each other again.

Wright set up his own architecture office in 1894 in Chicago and soon became well-known for his distinctive stylish residential designs. He specialized in low rise horizontally aligned bungalows that became known as 'Prairie Houses'. However, as an emerging architect, Wright could not afford to disagree over client's taste and also designed many more traditional dwellings but always tried to retain a significant element of his own innovative geometric styling in the design.

Wright relocated his studio to his home in 1898 to bring his work and family lives closer. This move made further sense as the majority of the architect's projects at that time were in Oak Park, Chicago where he lived or in nearby River Forest. The new Oak Park studio was one of Wright's first experiments with innovative architectural structure and became a compelling, much-admired advert for his business. By 1901, Wright had completed another 50 buildings, including many houses in Oak Park and the surrounding area.

"Youth is a circumstance you can't do anything about. The trick is to grow up without getting old."

The Prairie Houses suited the flat, low-lying land around Chicago and were credited as having the first open-plan interior designs that we regard today as 'modern living spaces'. Windows whenever

Fallingwater by Frank Lloyd Wright,
Bear Run, Pennsylvania, USA.

possible were long, and low. A style that was new to the west, but reflected Wright's interest in the architecture of Japan, where, in 1920, he built one of his most famous Prairie-style public buildings – the earthquake-proof, Imperial Hotel in Tokyo.

The Imperial Hotel design was widely criticized at the time for its use of the floating cantilever which was regarded as an unsafe feature. But Wright's design was totally vindicated in 1923 when a major earthquake struck Tokyo and his hotel was one of the few buildings to remain undamaged.

Other public buildings in the Prairie style included the Unity Temple in Oak Park and the Johnson Wax Research Tower in Racine, Wisconsin, one of his few tall buildings. Many architects consider the Unity Temple to be the world's first modern building, because of its unique construction of only one material – reinforced concrete. But perhaps his best-known masterpiece, which was 16 years (1943–59) in the making, is The Solomon R. Guggenheim Museum of Art in New York City.

Fallingwater is a house designed at Mill Run near Pittsburgh, Pennsylvania in 1939. A private countryside retreat built for Mr and Mrs Edgar J. Kaufman, it is regarded as another of Wright's masterpieces. Cantilevered out over the rock ledges of a waterfall and stream it blends in with the natural lines of the tall straight surrounding trees. Wright was always conscious of the setting of his buildings and designed them so they fitted naturally into their environment.

Wright also designed the Price Tower in Bartlesville, Oklahoma, which is one of the two existing vertically oriented Wright structures (the other being the Johnson Wax Tower mentioned above). Commissioned by the H. C. Price Company, a local oil and chemical firm, and completed in 1956, the Tower was designated a United States National Historic Landmark in 2007.

In 1911, Frank Lloyd Wright had designed his own house called Taliesin at Spring Green, Wisconsin and he later built Taliesin West, which became his winter home and studio complex in Scottsdale, Arizona from 1937 until his death in 1959 at the age of 91. Taliesin West continues today as the home of the Frank Lloyd Wright Foundation and the site of the Frank Lloyd Wright School of Architecture.

Frank Lloyd Wright's innovative designs were a major break with Victorian values and the traditional architecture of the 19th century. Wright's simple, clean-looking, low-pitched roofs and horizontal lines are now considered to be perfectly characteristic examples of 20th century architecture. Although many were constructed in the early years of the century, the creative, ground-breaking designs set the tone for the new millennium and paved the way for young architects such as Mies van der Rohe and Frank Gehry to follow in the footsteps of the master – Frank Lloyd Wright – the most influential architect in the last 100 years.

"Every great architect is – necessarily – a great poet. He must be a great original interpreter of his time, his day, his age."

MARK ZUCKERBERG

Making the World More Transparent

QUOTE

*"The thing that we are trying to do at Facebook,
is just to help people connect."*

BIOGRAPHY

NAME: Mark Elliot Zuckerberg

BORN: May 14, 1984
White Plains, New York,
United States

NATIONALITY: American

OCCUPATION: Computer programmer,
internet entrepreneur

Mark Zuckerberg, the co-creator of the social networking site Facebook, was born in White Plains, New York, in 1984. His father, Edward, was a dentist and his mother, Karen, was a psychiatrist. At high school, Mark developed a particular aptitude for classics; at Phillips Exeter Academy, he won prizes in classical studies and science. He was a star fencer also known for reciting lines from the *Iliad*.

He started using computers while at school. His father taught him BASIC programming in the 1990s, then hired software developer David Newman to give him private programming tuition. David Newman describes Zuckerberg as 'a prodigy': it was difficult to stay ahead of him. Zuckerberg enjoyed developing computer programs, communication tools in particular.

His father's dental practice was run from home, so Zuckerberg developed a software program called ZuckNet, to allow the computers at home and at the dental surgery to communicate with one another. This useful linking software was in reality a simplified, pioneer, version of AOL's Instant Messenger, which came out the following year.

Remembering this phase, Zuckerberg said, 'I had a bunch of friends who were artists. They'd come over, draw stuff, and I'd build a game out of it.' But his friends recognized that he was by no means a stereotypical geek – there was the fencing and the interest in Greek and Roman epics. He built a music player called the Synapse Media Player. This used artificial intelligence to build a profile of the listener's listening habits. Microsoft and AOL tried to buy Synapse. They tried to recruit Zuckerberg too, but he decided in 2002 to go to Harvard instead.

When he started at Harvard, where he studied psychology and computer science, Zuckerberg already had a reputation as a programming prodigy. He set up a program called CourseMatch, which allowed students to choose classes based on the choices of other students, and enabled them to set up study groups. Then, 'for fun', he created a program called Facemash, which allowed students to nominate the best-looking person from a choice of photos. The students had books that were called Face

Books, containing the names and pictures of everyone living in the student hall.

The Facemash site, where students were able to vote and produce a ranking, was based on this data. Within 48 hours the college had to shut the site down because its excessive use had overloaded Harvard's server, stopping more serious students from getting access to the Internet. Many students were also complaining that their rights had been infringed – their photos had been uploaded and used without their permission. It was a rite of passage for Zuckerberg, who made a public apology.

Zuckerberg's dorm at Harvard was the launchpad for Facebook itself in February 2004. It began as a purely 'Harvard thing', until Zuckerberg decided to open it to other universities. In this he was helped by his room-mate, Dustin Moskovitz, and Facebook spread to Stanford, New York, Cornell, Penn, Brown and Yale.

> *"It's almost a disadvantage if you're not on it now."*

The business potential of Facebook, as an advertising platform, was obvious. Zuckerberg moved to Palo Alto in California with Dustin Moskovitz and two other Harvard friends, Eduardo Saverin and Chris Hughes, taking a lease on a house that functioned as an office. Peter Thiel supplied capital for the new company. The group had planned to return to Harvard, but in the end stayed in California.

They had offers to buy Facebook from major corporations but decided to run it themselves. Zuckerberg said, 'It's not because of the amount of money. For me and my colleagues, the most important thing is that we create an open information flow for people.' In 2010 he repeated this view, 'The thing I really care about is the mission of making the world open.'

The popularity of Facebook as a social networking site was overwhelming. By the middle of 2010, Facebook had 500 million users. But there is another mission, which is making money. The site is a major platform for targeted advertising. Zuckerberg plays this side of Facebook down, saying that Facebook could have a lot more advertising; 'Look at how much of our page is taken up with ads compared to the average search query. The average for us is a little less than 10 percent of the pages and the average for search is about 20 percent taken up with ads … [Increasing the advertising is] the simplest thing we could do. But we aren't like that. We make enough money.'

Mark Zuckerberg has become very influential, by virtue of the huge number of people who use his site. In 2010 *Vanity Fair* magazine put him at the top of its Top 100 list of 'the most influential people of the Information Age'; *The New Statesman* ranked Zuckerberg 16th in its list of the world's 50 most influential people. He is thought to be the world's youngest multi-billionaire. Mark Zuckerberg joined Bill Gates and Warren Buffett in signing a 'Giving Pledge', a promise to donate over the course of time at least half of their wealth to charity.

Some people claim that Facebook networking was responsible for the revolutions in Tunisia and Egypt. The Tunisian revolution had a slow burn, with the organization Takriz starting as 'cyber think tank' in 1998: online discussion was considered safer than physical meetings. Over the next ten years more Tunisians gradually went online. By 2008, there were 30,000 Tunisian Facebook users: a year later there were 800,000 and by 2011 nearly 2 million. One of the revolutionaries described Facebook as 'the global positioning system for this revolution'.

Facebook probably played a less important role in the Egyptian revolution. The Egyptian revolt began later and very few Egyptians had Facebook accounts. But following the street murder of Khaled Said a Facebook Group was formed called 'We Are All Khaled Said'. In 2011 it had 1.5 million members. The extent of Facebook's (and therefore Mark Zuckerberg's) influence on the Arab Spring revolution will probably continue to be hotly debated.

In May 2012, Zuckerberg took Facebook public and floated the company on the stock market. But the flotation got off to a disastrous start as shareholders took fright over the company's initial valuation of $38 per share. Just three months after the flotation, the share price had collapsed to about $18, wiping $48 billion off the company's stock market value. Some accused Mark Zuckerberg of overhyping the company's growth forecasts. But the company's recent forecast-beating results have helped restore investor confidence and, in July 2013, the world's largest social networking site saw its price rise to the $38 flotation level for the first time since they began trading. Mark Zuckerberg currently has a net worth of an estimated $24 billion.

"By giving people the power to share, we're making the world more transparent."

This edition published in 2014 by
Chartwell Books
An imprint of Book Sales
A Division of Quayside Publishing Group, Inc.
276 Fifth Avenue, Suite 206
New York, New York 10001
USA

© 2014 Oxford Publishing Ventures Ltd
Spring Hill House, Spring Hill Road
Begbroke, Oxford OX5 1RX
England

ISBN-13: 978-0-7858-3117-4
ISBN-10: 0-7858-3117-7

Printed in China